MW01287469

INTO THE DMZ

A BATTLE HISTORY OF OPERATION HICKORY

May 1967, Vietnam

Mark A. Cauble

Eagle
Editions

2005

EAGLE EDITIONS
AN IMPRINT OF HERITAGE BOOKS, INC.

Books, CDs, and more – Worldwide

For our listing of thousands of titles see our website
at
www.HeritageBooks.com

Published 2005 by
HERITAGE BOOKS, INC.
Publishing Division
65 East Main Street
Westminster, Maryland 21157-5026

COPYRIGHT © 2005 Mark A. Cauble

All rights reserved. No part of this book may be reproduced or transmitted in any form or by any means, electronic or mechanical, including photocopying, recording or by any information storage and retrieval system without written permission from the author, except for the inclusion of brief quotations in a review.

International Standard Book Number: **0-7884-3361-X**

For those who were there

CONTENTS

PHOTOGRAPHS, MAPS AND ILLUSTRATIONS

Foreword

WOW! This history of war is a thriller! It is small unit combat at its best.

Mark Cauble has written a powerful, thoroughly documented post-mortem about war for his comrades at arms and for those who are eager to learn about realities of the Vietnam experience. He achieves this portrait by two editorial techniques. First, he summarizes the global spectrum of geopolitics and grand strategy by his opening and closing chapters in a sweeping, broad-view style of renowned historians. Then, he depicts the tactics and nature of war in a series of verbal snapshots from one violent battle, with their commentary in vernacular common to warriors of all generations.

Cauble's analysis of the Vietnam experience and his combat account of a horrendous ambush are based upon a combination of strict academic research and detailed eye witness reports including his own correspondence, unit diaries and command chronologies. He describes the raw courage of brutal small unit combat with detailed vivid accuracy in the words of its participants. The text flows rapidly in the actual words of the eyewitnesses. By using a continuous flow of citations, the reader becomes mentally and emotionally involved in a dialogue that illustrates the humanity of the combatants.

For the student of military history, *INTO THE DMZ* depicts the reality of war through Operation Hickory in May 1967. It reveals the consequences of hasty plans and orders. It deals with the snafus resulting from lack of stand-by combat support for rapid evacuation under fire; of mass casualties, on-call responsive delivery of supporting arms fire missions, and immediate resupply of water, beans and bullets. It also demonstrates the crucial power of properly trained Marines and sailors of small unit levels and billets to deal instantaneously with the unexpected reversals and the shock of surprise attacks, turning the tides of battle into victory.

For those members of the 2nd Battalion, 26th Marines and attached members of the 3rd Marine Division, *INTO THE DMZ* reunites the survivors and the deceased in the tale of their combat encounter and creates a vicarious reunion with their North Vietnamese enemy. It is another testament that for the individual warrior, war is limited to the world of his small unit and its firefight with the enemy. For the next of kin and descendants, relatives, friends and neighbors, this sensitive but brutal account unites them once again with loved ones in a thoughtful closure of their worst nightmare.

These warriors indeed earned the "red badge of courage" in the history of warfare!

Col. Duncan D. Chaplin III USMC (Ret.)

Author's Note

HISTORIANS AND PHILOSOPHERS are usually detached from the events and the ideas they describe, and eyewitness accounts of warfare are almost always written by officers. I do not know of another first-hand historical work whose author was a historian/philosopher/combat infantryman. This text therefore, has three voices instead of one.

My original intention was to be a historian and to leave my personal story out of the narrative. My own experiences were so disturbing that I did not want to revisit them. However, I soon realized that my memoirs were crucial to the book. I resolved the problem by referring to myself in the third person. This "trick" provided me with the necessary emotional protection. Finally, certain issues needed to be reflected on and I had to delve into philosophy.

These three voices give the work a unique perspective.

Author (*Author's Collection*)

Acknowledgments

I WOULD LIKE TO THANK Ramona L. Boyton for typing the manuscript. The manuscript readers also have my gratitude for their efforts. These important people are: Arlene Bryant, Richard Reeb, Dale Jensen, Clark Sarchet, Dick Dirk, Kim Young, Joann Jelly, Joseph A. Clark, Jerry and Sue Hotz, Joan and Bill Robb, Garland and Nancy Dittman, Jan and Ernie Stoll, and Jayne Wanner. Some of my fellow Marines also reviewed the text, they are: Duncan Chaplin, Robert Brown, Billy Mitchell, Richard Ross, and Roger Chicoine. Finally, I am lucky to be married to an understanding woman – I love you, Sue Ann.

Part I

Overture

The Slippery Slope

IT STARTED as a clash of ideas and ended as a political struggle. Along the way it involved a group of Marines fighting for their lives in the far-off jungles of Vietnam.

The communist movement and its conflict with the West began with Karl Marx and the publication of the *Communist Manifesto* in 1848. Marx believed the workers would inevitably rebel and overthrow the democratic countries of Western Europe. The proletariat, he said, would then establish a classless socialist state, which would develop into an ill-defined communist society.[1]

The execution of hostages and indiscriminate destruction of Paris during the Commune of 1871 was, Marx claimed, an example of the transitional form of government through which the working class would have to pass on the way to freedom.[2]

The excesses of the Commune horrified and opened the eyes of some people in the Western democracies. What would happen, they worried, if the Marxists were ever able to gain control of a whole country? Their worst fears were to become reality. During late 1917 communists, led by Vladimir Ilyich Lenin, overthrew Russian democracy, established the Red dictatorship (soon called the Union of Soviet Socialist Republics) and broke their World War I alliance with the Western Allies.[3] The West came to the aid of the Russian anti-communist Whites. The Whites were defeated and Joseph Stalin, who replaced Lenin as leader of the Soviet Union, systematically murdered seven million of his own people in order to solidify Red dominance.[4] The Soviet-Nazi Non-aggression Pact of 1939[5] and the communist invasion of Finland almost led to war between the Soviets and the West. Conflict was averted only by the Nazi conquest of France the next year.[6] Adolph Hitler's 1941 invasion of the Soviet Union put the Soviets on the side of the Allies.[7] It was an uneasy alliance, which the conflict over the post-war disposition of Poland would bring to an end.

The breach between the former friends was recognized four years later in Winston Churchill's Iron Curtain telegram, "...what is to happen about Russia? ...an Iron Curtain is drawn down...there seems little doubt that the whole of the regions east of the line...will soon be completely in their hands."

East Germany and all Eastern Europe, with the exception of Greece, fell under Marxist control.[8]

The Cold War had begun.

The Reds threatened to overrun both Western Europe and Asia. American Diplomat George F. Kennan's policy of containment became the accepted anti-Soviet strategy of the West. His article, published anonymously in *Foreign Affairs* magazine July 1947, said, "...It is clear that the main element of any United States policy toward the Soviet Union must be that of a long-term patient but firm and vigilant containment of Russian expansive tendencies.... Soviet power...bears within it the seeds of its own decay...."[9]

From 1945 to 1967 the West was successful in stopping the Reds in Berlin, Greece, Iran and South Korea, but failed in China and Cuba. Rebellions against communist rule in East Germany and Hungary were crushed without interference from the West.[10] The strategy of containment was also put to the test in Indo-China.

American entanglement in Vietnam was tied to France's involvement in the area. The French moved into Indo-China during the nineteenth century, but France's interest in the area dated to 1680, when it established a trading post in Vietnam.[11] A treaty with China in June 1885 gave France undisputed control of Indo-China,[12] but anti-French resistance persisted until World War II. During late 1940 the Japanese began occupying Indo-China.[13] Resistance by nationalist groups was now directed against the Japanese. The Marxists, led by Ho Chi Minh, emerged as the most effective anti-Japanese group and were supported by the Allies. The United States helped the Vietnamese communists with arms, munitions, food and advisors from 1942 to 1945. When the Japanese evacuated Indo-China, Ho declared Vietnam an independent state on September 2, 1945.[14] The French gave Ho the impression that they would acquiesce. Instead, they gathered their forces and moved back into Indo-China during the next year. The

Reds attacked the French in Hanoi December 19, 1946.[15]

This was the beginning of the Indo-China War.

The French defeated Ho, but the communists retreated into the jungle and continued the fight using guerrilla tactics. Ho's men were supplied by the Soviets and the Cold War placed the United States on the side of the French. The French attempt to draw the Marxists out of the jungle at Dien Bien Phu ended in disaster, and on May 7, 1954, after a valiant fifty-five-day struggle, the French surrendered.[16]

The French asked the United States to intervene with air power to save Dien Bien Phu, but President Dwight D. Eisenhower refused. He reasoned, "that the end result would be to drain off our resources" without solving the problem of "Red China itself."[17]

Historian of the war Bernard B. Fall maintained that even if America had used its air power, while it might have saved Dien Bien Phu, it would not have won the war. The French were destined to lose he said, because they could not prevent the flow of supplies from Red China to the communist Vietnamese and they did not have the backing of the Vietnamese population.[18] The French lost 75,867 men in Indo-China[19] and killed 400,000 communists.[20] That means the French killed more than five Indo-Chinese for every man they lost. But it was not enough.

Ho had told the French, "You can kill ten of my men for every one I kill of yours. But even at those odds, you will lose and I will win."[21]

The Geneva Accords were signed, ending the Indo-China War, on July 20, 1954.[22]

The Accords split Indo-China into North and South Vietnam, and Laos. North Vietnam was controlled by the Marxists, South Vietnam was temporarily held by the French, and Laos was declared neutral. There was to be a referendum to reunite North and South Vietnam in the summer of 1956.[23] To avoid a certain communist election victory, the United States intervened during 1955. A United States-sponsored government under Ngo Dinh Diem ruled South Vietnam after the French left and the unification vote never took place.[24] The communist Viet Cong began an insurgency in South Vietnam five years later[25] and the United States supplied South Vietnam with arms, munitions, food and advisors.

Despite a warning from French President Charles de Gaulle that Vietnam was "a bottomless military and political swamp,"[26] President John F. Kennedy sharply increased American advisors from less than 700 to 16,000 men.[27]

Kennedy concluded that the patriotic yet corrupt Diem would never achieve victory and he told South Vietnamese generals that the United States would cut off aid to South Vietnam if Diem stayed in power. Consequently the generals assassinated Diem on November 1, 1963.[28] The murder of Diem threw the country into chaos, and taking advantage of the situation, the Viet Cong attacked and were threatening to cut South Vietnam in half. When Kennedy was assassinated on November 22, 1963, Lyndon B. Johnson was elevated to the Presidency.[29]

Two weeks later, Johnson decided that American troops would be necessary to save South Vietnam from communist domination. Johnson believed the loss of South Vietnam would endanger his election bid, and the famous Tonkin Gulf incident provided him with the necessary cover for his planned intervention. Two North Vietnamese patrol boats attacked two American destroyers August 2-4, 1964, in the Tonkin Gulf. Congress obligingly passed the Tonkin Gulf Resolution three days later.

The Resolution authorized the President to "take all necessary measures to repel any armed attack against the forces of the United States and to prevent further aggression."

Johnson viewed this resolution as equivalent to a declaration of war and American combat troops began arriving in Vietnam March 1965. Over the next four years the number of American troops in Vietnam would steadily increase.[30]

The 1964 edition of Fall's *Street without Joy*, predicted that the American effort was doomed because the communists had a sanctuary from which to fight, as well as the support of the Vietnamese people.[31] His warning went unheeded.

The United States first bombed North Vietnam February 7, 1965, in response to a Viet Cong attack on American installations. American planes began continuous bombing of North Vietnam that same month.[32] Gradually, Johnson would increase the intensity of the bombing. Eight months later, the United States, in its first battle with the North Vietnamese Army, killed almost 2,000 in Ia Drang Valley. More than 300 Americans also died and the United States quickly abandoned the hard-won ground. American Commanding General William L. Westmoreland, as a result of this "victory," believed he could bleed the communists to death with search-and-destroy operations. He thought helicopter mobility and massive firepower would enable American troops to find and destroy the enemy.[33]

But the battle of Ia Drang had also taught the North Vietnamese how to fight American forces. They learned to counteract American firepower by staying close, within twenty meters of American units. They knew that the United States military would not call in fire that would endanger their own men. Additionally, the North Vietnamese would fight only when it was to their advantage. Their knowledge of the land and people made it possible for them to decide when and where combat would take place. At the beginning of a battle, they would lure American troops into their kill zones and engage the American units at extremely close range. After being attacked the Americans would fall back with their dead and wounded and pummel the enemy with artillery and air power. Cleverly, the North Vietnamese would often retreat before American firepower could pour death and destruction onto their positions.[34]

Not only was communist infiltration from North Vietnam unstoppable, it was increasing. The United States military was unable to kill the NVA soldiers faster than they could be replaced, and many officials realized the American public would not accept the growing number of United States casualties.[35] On December 18, 1965, presidential advisors told Johnson the war could not be won.

"'What you are saying,' Johnson interjected, 'is that no matter what we do militarily, there is no sure victory.'

"'That's right,' McNamara replied."[36]

Unfortunately, Johnson did not know how to disengage from the conflict. The United States had to continue its buildup in Vietnam just to keep the communists from overrunning the country.[37] The Americans would eventually have 542,000 men in Vietnam. Hoping for victory, United States search-and-destroy operations continued in Vietnam throughout 1966 and 1967.

United States Marine Maj. Gen. Victor Krulak disagreed with Westmoreland's strategy.[38] Krulak wrote a paper showing that the

North Vietnamese would win a war of attrition.[39] Instead, he said, the United States should "seek the support of the Vietnamese peasantry" and use American air power to blast the communist forces.[40] Initially the Marines followed this approach and they resisted[41] Westmoreland's pressure to seek out and destroy enemy units.[42] The North Vietnamese decided the issue by sending their 324 B Division "across the demilitarized zone in the summer of 1966."[43] Westmoreland forced the Marines to give up their pacification plan[44] and six Marine battalions were sent north to counter the enemy move across the DMZ.[45] Westmoreland had the Marines "establish a series of strong points along the DMZ" including Con Thien and Khe Sanh, and "Army artillery batteries of 175mm guns" were put into these fortified positions.[46]

Undetected, the North Vietnamese moved into the Khe Sanh area and spent three months fortifying their positions.[47] An NVA regiment occupied Hills 861 and 881 south, and 881 north near Khe Sanh, and another enemy regiment was held in reserve. The United States Marines, during late April 1967, were sent to take these hills. After two and a half weeks of bitter fighting, the Marines had their hills, but had paid dearly for them.[48] The NVA changed direction and moved against Con Thien.[49] The communist attack on Con Thien led to Operation Hickory. This operation provided a specific example of small unit tactics used during the Vietnam War by the United States Marine Corps and North Vietnamese forces. It also represented a major escalation of the war. Most importantly, this is a story of the courage and endurance of men in combat.

175mm gun (*USMC*)

Part II

Into the DMZ

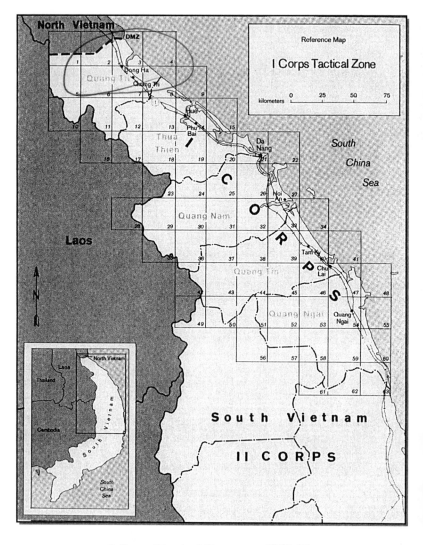

I Corps Tactical Zone map (*USMC*)

The hot, steaming scrambled eggs and steaks were plopped onto the Marines' mess tins. They were in the middle of the jungle, about to start what seemed to be another routine operation. The hot breakfast was a surprise. Several Marines just stared at their food.

Pfc Mark Cauble walked up and said, "What's the matter? You're not eating?"

They answered, "Don't you know what this means?"[1]

1

"We Might See Some Action"

May 15

During April 1967 the United States Marine Corps reinforced the 3rd Marine Division in the three northern provinces of South Vietnam. This was in response to recent concentrations of NVA in the Demilitarized Zone between North and South Vietnam. The additional troops were to come from the 1st Marine Division, and so the 26th Marine Regiment was transferred from the 1st Marine Division to the 3rd Marine Division. The 26th Marines moved from the 1st Marine Division area "to the vicinity of Phu Bai."[2]

This proved to be a prudent move because two Red battalions launched an assault on Con Thien on May 8, 1967. The attack was obviously timed to coincide with the anniversary of the surrender of French troops at Dien Bien Phu in 1954. Con Thien was critical to the enemy because it provided excellent observation of the DMZ. The United States also recognized the position's importance and had a reinforced Marine Battalion defending Con Thien. The NVA penetrated the American perimeter and engaged the American troops in close combat.[3] After five hours of intense fighting the Marines were able to repel the attack. One hundred and ninety-seven North Vietnamese bodies lay in and around the Leatherneck entrenchments. American losses were also heavy, with 44 killed and 110 wounded.[4]

The NVA were using the DMZ to stage attacks on American forces, and Washington authorized ground action in the southern half of the DMZ. The mission was to engage and destroy enemy forces and to evacuate all civilians. Three operations were designed to accomplish these tasks: Beau Charger, Belt Tight and Lam Son 54. These combined operations were to start on May 18.[5] Meanwhile, the 3rd Marine Division was still conducting Operation Prairie IV, which had started April 20.[6] The North Vietnamese ambushed the 2nd Battalion, 26th Marines during Prairie IV. Operation Hickory was launched to save 2/26 and trap the enemy.

Capt. Frank D. Fulford, the tough and professional commanding officer of Echo Company, 2/26, said the company commanders were first notified they were going into the DMZ about May 13. The battalion had just finished two weeks on Operation Shawnee.[7] According to Pfc. Billy Mitchell, the grunts (Marine riflemen so called because the weight of their equipment made them grunt[8]) of Golf Company were told the next day, that the battalion, "would be going on an operation in the DMZ for a period of twelve to fourteen days" and it would begin May 15.[9]

Fox Company's Jerry Dallape figured trouble was ahead:

> It was the middle of May 1967 and Fox Company 2/26 had been sent to Phu Bai. We usually would have had a few hours to relax and resupply, but today's resupply was on the top of the list before anything else. All the supplies we needed were present in great amounts; crates of new M-16 ammo, cases of hand grenades and belts of machine gun ammo were neatly stacked for our use. We received new field utilities, ample rations and water. We had everything that you could ask for if you were going on a big operation, but no one said anything about a big operation. Now everyone knows that the Marine Corps never gives you anything that it does not expect you to use and here we were with enough supplies to fight World War III.[10]

The approximately 1,000 men of 2/26 were told at dawn May 15, that they were to embark on a sixteen-day operation.[11] The number cited of Marines in 2/26 is a best estimate as exact figures for that day do not exist.

A full-strength Marine battalion numbered 1,193 men. The battalion was divided into four 216-man rifle companies, and a headquarter and service company. The H & S company contained both 106mm recoilless rifles and 81mm mortars. A rifle company had 210 men and six officers, divided into three rifle platoons of forty-six men and one lieutenant. The company also had a weapons platoon with three 60mm mortars, three M-60 machine guns and three rocket launchers. A lieutenant commanded the weapons platoon, but it was usually divided up and attached to the rifle platoons. There was also a small headquarters comprised of a captain, a lieutenant (who served as executive officer), a first sergeant, a gunnery sergeant, an armorer, a supply sergeant and administrative clerks. The rifle platoons were each led by a lieutenant, who had a staff sergeant as his second-in-command. Each platoon had three rifle squads and a command group. The command group consisted of the lieutenant, the staff sergeant, a right guide, a radio operator and a corpsman (U.S. Naval medical personnel attached to the Marines). The rifle squads were led by a sergeant and totaled fourteen men. Thirteen men carried M-16 rifles and one carried an M-79 grenade launcher. The squad was divided into three four-man fire teams. The number of Marines in a battalion fluctuated and it was usually below full strength.[12] During May 1967, 2/26 averaged thirty-seven officers, 1132 men and fifty-five Naval personnel.[13] Billy Mitchell remembered that Golf Company had 197 men at the start of the battle.[14] Using that figure and multiplying by four rifle companies, we arrive at an estimate of 800 riflemen. The balance of the battalion was headquarters and support personnel.

The United States Marine Corps is a world famous elite fighting unit that was established by the Second Continental Congress on November 10, 1775.[15] The officers and men were rigorously trained and had an outstanding *esprit de corps*. The Leathernecks all went through ten weeks of boot camp and the riflemen received four additional weeks of combat training.[16] For Marines, the tour in Vietnam was thirteen months.[17] 2/26 had been in Vietnam since August 1966 and participated in four previous operations: Prairie II, Prairie III, Canyon and Shawnee.[18] It would take all of the grunts' spirit, experience, and training to get them through the upcoming battle.

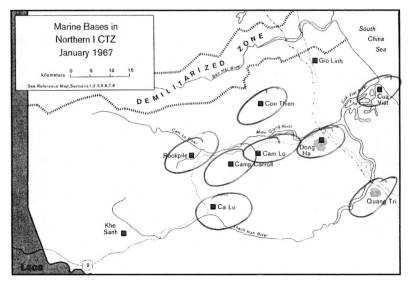

Marine Bases in Northern I CTZ map (*USMC*)

ME WITH MY MACHINE GUN

Billy Mitchell (*Mitchell Collection*)

The battalion boarded forty-five trucks[19] at 0800Hours[20] and moved from Phu Bai to Dong Ha. Twenty-three-year-old Mitchell had just been promoted to machine gunner, but was not expecting a lot of action. "We were at the DMZ in March on Prairie III and didn't run into much."

Mitchell said, some Marines heard Capt. Samuel Oots, the fatherly and innovative commanding officer of Golf Company, say that he thought there would be action. Oots said he would try to keep casualties down by eliminating suspected enemy positions with artillery fire. Jesse Fields, a six-foot four-inch, 240-pound native of Louisiana, was Mitchell's assistant machine gunner and "bodyguard." Each Marine in Golf was given six c-ration meals and the option of wearing a flak jacket. At the time, the Leathernecks were issued M-55 plated body armor,[21] which weighed nine pounds.[22] Mitchell decided not to carry a flak jacket because, "it was so hot."[23]

The truck drive of May 15 is still remembered by Dallape:

> The next day after a quick breakfast the whole company loaded up on trucks to form a large convoy. What we didn't realize was that the entire battalion had moved out with us. We headed North up Highway One through the city of Hue. The city of Hue was always full of people on motorbikes and bicycles hurrying from place to place. It was full of pretty young girls who were middle class in dress. There was even a university with Vietnamese co-eds. I always liked traveling through Hue, but I didn't like anything that lay to the north of the city. On this trip we were to go a lot farther north than any of us had ever gone. At the end of the day the convoy pulled into Dong Ha. Dong Ha had been receiving artillery fire from inside the DMZ. The night before we arrived they had been hit pretty hard. No one was out and about unless they had to be.[24]

The weather created an ominous feeling about the operation for South Carolina native Mitchell during the drive to Dong Ha: "It had been raining and was a real dreary day." Seeing all the Marines moving north also changed his mood. "Now we were beginning to realize we might see some action."[25]

81mm mortar (*Brown Collection*)

60mm mortar (*DOD*)

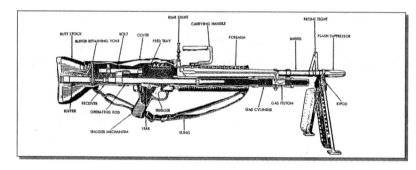

M-60 machine gun (*DOD*)

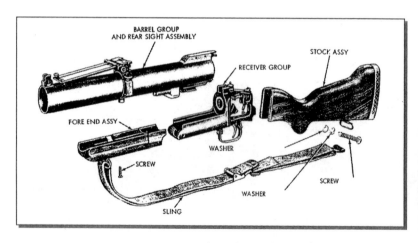

M-79 grenade launcher (*DOD*)

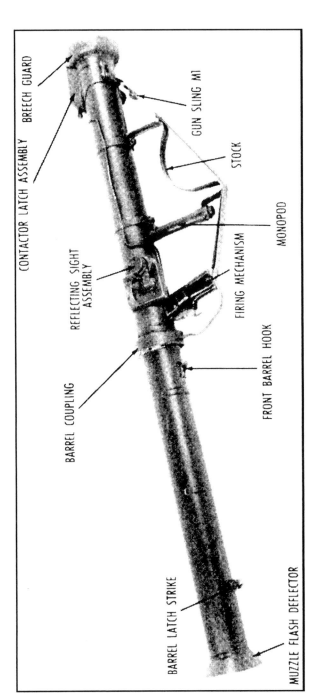

3.5-inch rocket launcher (*USMC*)

After arriving at Dong Ha, the battalion staff met with regimental commander Col. John J. Padley at 1600H.[26] The mission of 2/26 was to move north of Cam Lo and join Operation Prairie IV, which was already in progress.[27] After a two-hour holdover at Dong Ha, the battalion crossed over the Cam Lo River.[28]

This second phase of the truck drive also remained vivid to Dallape:

> Hurry up and wait. Squad leaders were trying to get everyone on the right truck. We were all trying to gather all our gear while wolfing down our morning c-rat delights. It seemed like everyone was dashing from one place to another for little or no purpose, but we all finally managed to settle down in the proper truck. The convoy finally rumbled out through the concrete barrels that marked the outside of the perimeter.
>
> We headed down the infamous Highway Nine. The French had battled along this highway many times and this time it was our turn. Our trip was fast, maybe an hour at the most.
>
> Our truck stopped near a small group of 9th Marines and we dismounted. I asked one of the Marines what was going on. He said a couple of days ago there had been a big firefight somewhere up ahead off a dirt road leading to a village. He said that he had heard that the VC were dug-in near the village. It was now apparent to me that this was going to be our objective.[29]

As they drove north, the Americans were discussing what they would be up against.

Bill Hancock of Hotel Company wrote:

> I remember when we were on the trucks on the way up there that the NCOs (Non Commissioned Officers) and men who had been in Viet Nam longer than I, were saying that if we met the NVA it would be a different kind of fight than what we had encountered before. The VC usually broke off contact quickly, the NVA would try to get close to avoid

artillery and air strikes and fight it out until it was no longer in their favor.[30]

Leaving the trucks behind, Echo Company took the point and led the battalion for about 4000 meters to a bivouac site, arriving at around 1930H that evening. For this operation the men in 2/26 were required to take an entrenching tool, and as soon as the battalion stopped for the night, everyone started digging in. The night passed without incident.[31]

That evening 2/26 was reinforced with M-48 tanks. These tanks were armed with a turret-mounted 90mm cannon, a 50-caliber and a 30-caliber machine gun.[32] They were fully tracked and heavily armored.[33] Also arriving were Ontos, lightly armored, fully tracked anti-tank vehicles armed with six coaxially mounted 106mm recoilless rifles.[34] All of these armored vehicles were employed in the line. The tanks were Company A, 3rd Tank Battalion, commanded by Capt. B. F. Ennis. Capt. R. E. Byrne officered the Ontos from Company C, 3rd Anti-Tank Battalion.[35] Later that night, the professorial and business-like battalion commanding officer, Lt. Col. Charles R. Figard, called the company commanders together for a briefing.[36] The battalion sent out patrols. After his patrol returned, Joe Francis of Foxtrot reported to his platoon commander. He told his lieutenant that there was a lot of enemy activity ahead and that they had better move slow the next day or the battalion would walk into an ambush.[37]

Mitchell, Fields (*Mitchell Collection*)

Operation Hickory—M-48 tank (*Brown Collection*)

Ontos (*USMC*)

2

"Fix Bayonets and Stand By for Action"

May 16

THE MORNING OF MAY 16, the sun came up and enveloped the Marines in a blistering wave of heat. The temperature was to register 106° that day.[1] The grunts felt like they would drown in the humidity. Sweat poured off their bodies.[2]

The countryside was flat, with open fields surrounded by hedgerows, perfect defense positions for the NVA. The hedgerows were taller than a person and thick with vegetation, but the men advanced, chopping their way through them.[3]

The troops marched north on a dirt road only one lane wide, with trees and hedgerows on each side. A small white church with a grey roof and a bell tower provided the only relief in the jungle-induced, hazy yellow-green atmosphere.[4]

The Leathernecks' equipment, food, weapons and ammunition weighed about 100 pounds.[5] Marine riflemen normally wore olive-green jungle utilities and jungle boots and carried an olive-green helmet, pack, cartridge belt, flak-jacket, first aid kit, 200 rounds of rifle ammunition, six c-ration meals, two canteens, entrenching tool, two or more grenades, one or more pop-up flares, 60mm mortar shell, 3.5-inch rocket launcher round or 100 bullets of machine gun ammunition, and, of course, the brand new 5.56mm semi- or full-automatic M-16 assault rifle with five twenty-round magazines.

A month earlier, 2/26 was given the M-16 rifle to replace the beloved M-14. The sights were poor, and the bullet would drop sharply after traveling 300 yards. The worst problem was that it would often jam. The men were not happy with the new weapon and wished they had the excellent M-14 rifle back.[6]

The battalion moved up the road with Echo in the lead. The Alpha command group with Figard was in trace of Echo. Foxtrot followed Echo's lead. The Bravo command group, with executive officer Maj. James H. Landers, was in line with Golf, which was next in formation. Bringing up the rear of the column was Hotel.[7] Initially, Echo was supposed to move to the first checkpoint, and then Foxtrot was to pass through and take the advance. However, because of the good progress Echo was making, and the pressure to stay on schedule, Figard decided to let Echo continue in front.[8]

Dallape, again, has a very detailed memory of the march:

> The dirt road lay just in front of me. 3rd Platoon was lead element. Then 2nd Platoon followed. Our platoon, the first of Fox, fell in at the end in single file. There were troops falling in line behind us. I think it was Golf Company. There were also mechanized vehicles on our flanks. This was not good. We had to be going after something really big to have tracked vehicles with us.
>
> As we moved up the dirt road the terrain became lush. Not heavy jungle but green full pockets of trees separated by squares of dry rice paddies. The column stretched out along the road for miles.[9]

Water was a problem for the Americans from the beginning. The first check point was a creek and the Marines used the water from it to resupply their canteens.[10]

"We crossed a small stream," wrote the low-key Mitchell, "where bulldozers were building a road. The water was almost mud. We were out of water, so we filled our canteens with this muddy water."[11]

Broad-shouldered Cauble walked a number of yards upstream to avoid the muddy water, and filled both of his canteens. The brook, he remembered, was waist deep and cold. The earth-moving vehicles were with the grunts to widen the road for 175mm Army artillery.[12] Crossing the creek, Echo ran into men from 1/9, who had received mortar fire over the last few days. They told Fulford to keep their vehicles off the road because it was mined. Echo had five tanks moving with them.[13]

"By now," said Mitchell, "we were passing through what was left of 1/9. I remember a corpsman told me I was going to wish I had a flak jacket."[14]

As soon as Fulford's men crossed the stream, they moved off the road to the right and started paralleling it.[15]

Perez with M-14 (*Brown Collection*)

Author with M-16 (*Author's Collection*)

As the day wore on, it got hotter and the grunts started to run out of water. When Echo reached the second check point, Fulford asked Figard if they should continue at the head of the column or hold up and let another company pass through. The battalion commander decided that Echo should continue with the point.[16] Around 1100H Echo came up to what was commonly called "the firebreak." The firebreak was "a cleared swath 600 meters wide."[17]

The time of 1100H is a reasonable deduction. Different sources give conflicting time estimates. The Command Chronology says the ambush started four hours later[18] and Fulford says Echo arrived at the firebreak about 1400H.[19] Two accounts, 1st Platoon diary, Golf Company and John D. Giordano of Echo say Foxtrot was ambushed at noon.[20] The first air strikes in support of Foxtrot were thirty minutes later.[21] This supports the 1200H time frame. Moving back from this point, the estimate of arriving at the firebreak around 1100H seems reasonable. This is also the conclusion reached by the official USMC history.[22]

First Platoon, Echo Company was the point element and all five tanks were with it. When the Marines got about halfway across the firebreak, some NVA fired two rocket-propelled grenades at the tanks, but missed. The 2nd Platoon was sent forward, passed the head of the column and deployed in skirmish order (men on line, five meters apart). The Leathernecks then swept the area. Suddenly, there were about four airbursts from enemy 82mm mortars. The 2nd Platoon's sweep failed to make contact. Fulford reported this information to Figard.[23]

The battalion commander recommended a pullback by Echo to the south side of the firebreak. The CO told Fulford he was ordering Foxtrot forward to take up position on Echo's left flank. The two companies would then cross the firebreak together.[24]

Francis was not happy with the formation Foxtrot took as they moved forward. "We were ordered to pick up the pace and to pull in our flank security and advanced point. That was a major mistake or blunder."[25]

Golf's hard-charging and aggressive executive officer, 2nd Lt. Robert Brown, also wondered why the flank security was brought in. "We were…moving in column, with no flank security, when we got hit."[26]

Harold Fosmo, Jr., one of Landers's radio operators, recalled Landers's reaction to the order to pull-in security, "I do remember the Lt. Col. ordering the flanks pulled-in before we got hit and that Maj. Landers was upset by the order."[27]

Doubtless Figard thought the area was clear of the enemy, since Echo had already swept through it, and he wanted to reinforce his lead element as quickly as possible.

Fosmo had a high opinion of Landers: "Maj. Landers was the best officer I ever served with. He treated enlisted men with respect. He was tall and thin with reddish hair. He had a mustache and every morning he used saddle soap to twist it out. Walking behind him you could see the mustache sticking out past each side of his head."[28]

Waiting to strike the advancing Marines were 900-1200 North Vietnamese soldiers[29] of the 5th and 6th Battalions,[30] 812th Regiment,[31] 324 B Division.[32] Most likely, a third Red battalion, with another 450 to 600 men, was being held in reserve.[33]

An NVA battalion was divided into a headquarters, three infantry companies, one support company and a specialist company (signal, reconnaissance and sapper). The strength varied from 450 to 600 men. Each infantry company had 60 to 130 men and was organized into three platoons and a headquarters. Their platoons were split into three nine-man squads and each squad was further divided into three three-man cells. The infantry company carried AK-47 and SKS rifles, RPD 7.62mm machine guns and RPGs. The battalion's support company was equipped with 82mm mortars, 57mm and 75mm recoilless rifles, and 12.7mm heavy machine guns. This support company was usually split up and attached to the infantry companies.[34]

The enemy infantrymen usually wore a green cotton uniform with green boots that resembled high-top tennis shoes and carried the following: tan sun helmet, green pack, canteen, entrenching tool, ineffective stick-handled potato masher grenades, green or tan chest pouch which held three thirty-round AK-47 magazines, and the durable, reliable 7.62mm semi- or full-automatic AK-47 assault rifle.[35]

The enemy was well-entrenched.[36] Their defense system was self-sufficient and consisted of camouflaged, mutually supporting bunkers.[37] These battlements were heavily reinforced and capable of holding up to eight men. Sometimes, they would place 12.7mm heavy machine guns inside these fieldworks. The earthworks had a half-moon trench and this trench provided firing positions for the North Vietnamese. The dugouts were also surrounded by smaller positions called spider holes.[38] The enemy ramparts were only eighteen to twenty inches above ground. Consequently, they had low fields of fire and the Marines suffered a lot of head wounds.[39] The enemy would place these bunkers in extremely thick terrain and were, as we will see, undetectable until the grunts were right next to them.[40]

The NVA soldiers, said Oots, were all in extremely good condition. Their uniforms, equipment and weapons were clean and in good shape.[41]

"They were…stockier and in better condition than the Viet Cong I had seen," said Hancock.[42]

The North Vietnamese Army, which called itself the People's Army of Vietnam, was well trained and had decades of fighting experience.[43] Its recruits spent three months learning the basics of infantry fighting.[44] They were tough, motivated fighters.

The NVA troops were in two positions, one on either side of the firebreak. North of the firebreak they were arranged in an intricate U-shaped breastwork, which would strike the Leathernecks with converging fire from three different directions when they entered it. To the south they used the less elaborate L configuration, from which they sprayed death from two angles. The NVA would use the U defense whenever terrain permitted.

Each north and south bulwark was further divided into two lines, at least fifty meters apart. This gave them the option of retreating to another prepared area when hard pressed. Also, if our troops broke through their first line, and the enemy didn't leave, our men would be shot at from both front and rear when they tried to take the second line. The enemy could prepare these entrenchments in as little as two hours. When time allowed they would construct a third defensive belt.

Highly respected Vietnam War authority, Col. David H. Hackworth, commented on the effectiveness of these positions, "I have concluded that it is impossible to penetrate, flank, or envelop these fortifications without taking extremely heavy casualties."[45]

Robert Brown (*Brown Collection*)

mac
2004

NVA 82mm mortar

The enemy's plan, as events show, was to draw 2/26's forward company, Echo, into a trap and simultaneously to split the column with a second ambush. The enemy would then launch a double envelopment that would encircle and destroy the Marine battalion. The four airburst 82mm mortar rounds were, most likely, a signal to execute their plan. Fulford's caution ruined their scheme.

The God of War's maw opened wide.

The North Vietnamese south of the firebreak, their heads wrapped with cloth to protect them from explosive concussion,[46] calmly waited for Foxtrot to enter their L-shaped defense position. As Foxtrot rushed forward, Dallape recalled how the ambush, in the middle of the battalion, started:

> 3rd Platoon was at the head of the column and had already passed through the village. We passed a few grass huts and then came to an old Catholic church. There was a boy of about ten standing outside the church. We moved slowly down the road. We could see a small group of Vietnamese women and children behind the church hurrying out of sight. It seemed out of character to see them move so quickly. Suddenly, like a knife piercing the silence, the church bells rang. We could hear small arms fire break out immediately to our front in the direction of 3rd Platoon. We got down into defense positions and waited for orders to move out. 3rd and 2nd Platoons were under fire and could not move. The order came down to try to circle to our right and outflank the enemy. I was in the first squad of 1st Platoon and our adrenalin was pumping to its max. We heard that 3rd Platoon was taking heavy casualties and at least one machine gunner was dead. 2nd platoon was under lighter fire, but still couldn't move.[47]

Being touched by enemy weapons is horrifying. When a person is hit by a bullet, it is as though someone has run full-force and tackled him. The sudden impact takes his breath away and the blood pours out of the wound like hot soup splashing on his skin. Shrapnel from mortar and artillery shells is red hot when it hits someone. Just a small piece can dismember and throw his torn body into the air. For those who are wounded there are both visible and invisible scars. The injured body may heal, but the mental torment is more difficult to overcome.[48]

Corpsman Rainman remembered:

I was in the center of the ambush with Fox Company 3rd Platoon. We got hit after we left the village. My Lt. sent out guns after we got a few sniper rounds. I guess he thought he would swipe away the riff raff and drive on. They were totally exposed when they sprung the ambush...I got caught out in the field treating a Marine who was hit in the femur. We were pinned down out there. I got hit and... I got a Silver Star that day and I still don't know why.[49]

The information at the time was that the fight was triggered by an enemy sniper with an automatic rifle. The sniper started the ambush by taking out the lead fire team. The NVA had also placed a machine gun so that it could shoot straight down the road. When it opened fire the men of Foxtrot took cover right into booby-traps and preplanned fire zones.[50]

"There was a berm on both sides of the road and I believe that saved a lot of lives," said Ron Wickersham, who was with the Alpha command group and was carrying a radio for 81mm mortars.[51]

Larry Faulkner was the squad leader for the 2nd Squad, 3rd Platoon, Francis recalled, and when the ambush started:

All at once Faulkner was getting his men in position and trying to find them cover, while he himself was laying down cover fire for his squad and the rest of the platoon. All the while he himself was exposed to a hail of fire, he got his men cover, but he himself got hit several times by automatic rifle fire, killing him instantly. I saw him and several others go down at the same time. Cpl. Hall was one of them.[52]

Francis added:

Faulkner always talked about going back to Ohio. He always maintained that he married the finest woman in all of Ohio, which he always pronounced like it had an a on the end of it (like Ohia). He was about five feet seven inches tall, about 160 lbs, dark curly hair and kinda deep-set eyes and always had a day's growth on his face. Very soft spoken and one of the easiest going people that I have ever met, he always found a reason to smile; even in the worst of times he would find an air of optimism that gave you some light at the end of the tunnel. He talked of going to Ohio State when he got back home. But that was not meant to be for him and a lot of other good people that we lost on that one operation.[53]

After the NVA started the ambuscade, Dallape's 1st Platoon moved to the right to try to flank the enemy's position. Dallape remembered what happened:

"Move out!" That was the last thing I wanted to hear. We moved to the other side of the road. My heart was beating in my ears. We began moving rapidly in single file through a lightly wooded area lined with banana trees and hedgerows. It was hard to breathe. Our pace began to slow as we reached a well-manicured path, which was lined with banana trees on both sides. We could hear heavy firing just ahead of us and we paused as we began to receive a few stray rounds from the embattled 3rd Platoon area. I noticed the broad leaves of the banana trees rustle in the breeze as we lay there on the path. The bright rays of the sun filtered through them creating a strange light show.

First squad began to move slowly up the path followed by the 2nd and then the 3rd squad. We came upon a dead VC face down with his hands hidden under his body. His short coal-black hair was parted by a small trickle of blood. He wore a new well-kept uniform. He was not a VC, he was an NVA soldier. The people we had been fighting to the south were VC peasants. They were highly motivated hit and run guerrillas, but for the most part poorly trained and armed. The NVA were a different story. They had the best Chinese and Russian equipment and they would hold their positions and fight. I wanted to turn him over to see if he had a weapon, but we knew in many cases they booby-trapped their dead.

North Vietnamese Army

NVA AK-47

NVA 7.62mm heavy machine gun

North Vietnamese bunker

NVA 12.7mm heavy machine gun

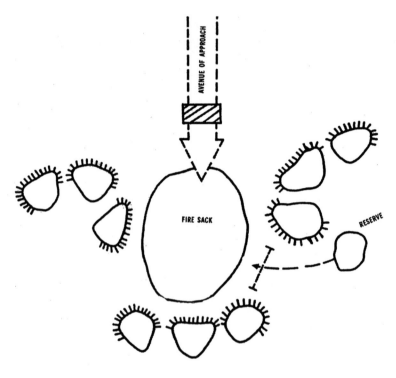

NVA "U" ambush (*U.S. Army*)

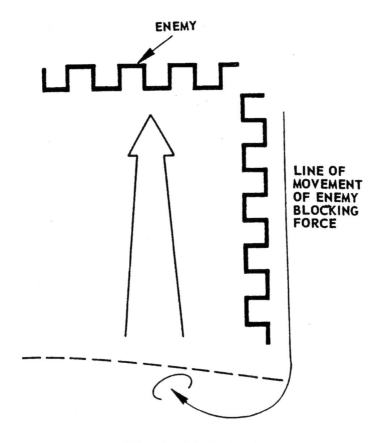

NVA "L" ambush (*U.S. Army*)

The word was passed back quietly from Marine to Marine to move out at double time. Our slow pace turned into a trot. The seventy pounds of gear I was carrying made running impossible. My legs burned and my lungs were ready to burst. We broke out of the banana grove and into a small clearing. The banana grove swept up along our left flank and there was a tree line straight ahead. There was a slight opening in the tree line. I couldn't go any farther with a full pack. I dropped the pack that was full of goodies from home, delicacies seldom found in the jungles we lived in, hard salami, cans of shoestring potatoes and other exotic foods but they had to go. I never did see that pack again.

We continued to walk and run through the opening in the tree line and into an open dry rice paddy. It was a wide-open square bordered with trees on all sides. The point man started to cross the open area with the rest of the squad behind him, but before he could reach the other side, the entire tree line erupted in small arms fire. Our gun team was half way across the paddy, caught in the open with no place to hide. The sounds were deafening, rounds were whizzing through the air all around us. We automatically dropped to the ground. It was impossible to tell where the shooting was coming from. It seemed to be coming from everywhere. Goodie was our Gun Squad Leader. He stared firing into the tree line to our right front. Gocknier was the gunner. He started firing the machine gun in the same direction. Hathay, the ammo carrier, was about ten steps in back of us. I started to open boxes of belt ammo and attach them to the machine gun. Goodie rolled on to his left side and started to say something to us, when a bullet ripped through his lower back and came out through his hip. His body lurched towards us and he made a loud dog like whimper and immediately fell perfectly still. Goodie lay face down a few yards away. The battle was in full force, raging all around us. We couldn't do anything for Goodie. We had to keep firing The Gun. In the first few seconds, half of the first squad was either dead or wounded. Those of us that weren't injured were firing back at a furious pace.

2nd Squad had not yet entered the dry rice paddy and 3rd Squad was behind them. They were spared the initial carnage. Then 2nd and 3rd Squad made a dash to try and support us as we provided covering fire. They were being cut down as they tried to move up. A corpsman made it to Goodie and placed a field dressing on him. When he finished, he ran towards another fallen Marine. I turned just in time to see a bullet shatter his right elbow, travel the length of his arm and blow out the rifle butt of his M-16. The impact of the round caused a spray of white styrofoam fill from the rifle butt to mingle with the corpsman's blood, producing a momentary red and white fog. It appeared as if someone had smashed a watermelon with a sledgehammer.[54]

Lance Cpl. David A. Fisch saw a Marine hit by enemy fire ten yards in front of an NVA bunker. He moved across an open area, under dense enemy automatic fire, with grenades exploding all around him. Fisch reached the wounded Marine and started to drag him to safety. As he was moving his comrade, he was killed by enemy fire. For this courageous act, he was posthumously awarded the Silver Star.[55]

Meanwhile, Dallape was still engaged in an intense firefight:

When I turned back, I saw that Glock had stopped firing and was lying motionless. The dirt was being churned up as rounds impacted all around us. I crawled over to Glock. I was sure he was dead. I poked him in the ribs and said, "Are you dead, man?"

He slowly turned to me and said, "It went through my helmet." His eyes were wide and staring, like a wild animal's eyes frozen by the headlights of a car.

I inspected his helmet and found a perfectly round hole at the top of it. I asked, "Are you hit?"

He answered slowly, "No, It went through my helmet."

I yelled above the fusillade of gunfire, "Then start shooting!" Later we learned that the round had entered the front of his helmet passed between the liner and the outside steel shell, and exited to the rear without ever hitting a hair on his head.

The round had gone into the pack he was carrying on his back. The only casualty here was a can of peach halves that resided in Glock's pack. It was just like you see in the movies but this was no movie. It was real as reality can get. Yet, it all flowed in slow motion as if we were in some gray surreal fog. It was an odd mixture of exquisite paralyzing fear and driving adrenalin. Everything was one mass of sound and confusion with no form or substance and yet some things were as clear as the finest crystal. It was these crystallized moments that would stay with me for the rest of my life.

Glock began firing again and I went back to feeding the machine gun. Overhead we could hear a Medevac helicopter coming in from our right. It was popping and sputtering black smoke from the exhaust pipe. It must have been called in for the casualties they were taking in 3d Platoon. It quickly flew out of sight to what must have been its inevitable crash site. The NVA had 50-caliber machine gun batteries that were chewing up anything that flew into their gun sights. It was going to be hard to get any type of air support.

Glock stopped firing again. This time the gun was jammed. He pulled the bolt back and let it go home but it still wouldn't fire. He opened the feed tray and found a spent piece of shell casing, which he cleared from the breach. I repositioned the ammo belt and Glock slammed the gun's cover plate down. Click, click; it still wouldn't fire. We reopened the weapon and this time we could see that another piece of brass was preventing the bolt from operating. Glock tried to get his finger into the breach to clear the gun but his fingers were just too large for the job. The sweat was rolling down my face as the time passed. Every second we were out of action gave the enemy more time to decimate our squad. Finally we turned the gun upside down and shook it violently. The round tumbled to the ground. There was no time to congratulate ourselves on clearing the weapon. We immediately got back to loading and firing a constant stream of rounds into the tree line.

Another gun team had come up on our left. They were locked in a deadly game of cat and mouse with two NVA soldiers, who were defending from a well-camouflaged spider trap. Gus, the main gunner for that gun team, was firing point blank into the NVA position, but every time the gun paused the NVA soldiers would pop out of their hole and throw grenades which would barely miss their mark. The gun team would manage to roll out of the way each time and return to laying down a barrage of machine gun fire. The gun was barking and then the grenades would explode. It seemed like they were locked into some bizarre mating dance. Gus finally changed his rhythm just enough to catch the NVA as they emerged from the hole. A long burst of the machine gun fire caught both NVA defenders in the chest, throwing them back into the den from which they emerged. I am not sure who was more surprised, Gus or the NVA soldiers.

Then we heard a deep rumbling noise coming from behind us. The clank and squeaking of metal tanks drew to a halt. The tank's cannon roared as it sent a round into a tree line. A deep-throated explosion ripped branches and earth into the air. Cpl. Curly was on his feet trying to get the attention of the tank commander in order to direct the tank's fire into specific enemy hot spots. Lt. Long was also on his feet motioning for the tank to follow his directions. The tank driver wasn't sure who to respond to since both were pointing in different directions. The competition for the tank's fire mission suddenly ended when Long went down. He was hit in the foot by an NVA bullet and was writhing in agony. Now, Curly had the full attention of the tank commander, but it was too late. Suddenly a loud whoosh was heard and something streaked past Curly. A rocket-propelled grenade exploded against the hull of the tank. Pieces of metal flew in all directions. The tank's engine roared as it backed out of the area. Even though the exterior armor of the tank had repelled the first rocket attack, it wasn't sticking around to risk another hit.[56]

After Long was wounded, Cpl. Ronald T. Curly, Squad Leader of the 1st squad, Company F, took charge of the platoon. Curly organized the defense and moved into the clear to better direct the platoon's weapons. Over a three-hour period he continuously exposed himself to enemy fire. Twice, by himself, he assaulted and destroyed enemy bunkers. Curly moved over the battlefield, encouraging his men, giving out ammunition and taking care of the wounded. Amazing as it may seem, he was unharmed by enemy bullets. For his valiant leadership against overwhelming odds, he was awarded the Navy Cross.[57]

The NVA now took the offensive. It swept around the right flank of Foxtrot, taking control of the road between Foxtrot and Golf. The battalion was split and Foxtrot was pretty much surrounded. Francis described Fox Company's perilous situation:

> …We took immediate casualties and got pinned down real good. The battalion was cut in half in such a way that no one could move to help anyone. Shit flew the better part of the day. Your company was being cut to pieces by automatic fire trying to get where we were. Mortars, rockets, machine guns, you name it, we were getting it. You wondered how in the hell you could stay alive with all that shit coming at you all at once. We kept regrouping and trying to makeup our teams, as we were getting wasted; they came pretty close to overrunning us.[58]

During the interval, Dallape remembered that he was still fighting the enemy:

> I don't know what the Ontos crew was thinking when they charged into the clearing. Were they bravely coming to our rescue or just sadly misinformed? But before it could fire any of its six guns another RPG streaked from the tree line and found its mark on the Ontos. The initial explosion was followed by explosion after explosion. The entire Ontos was in flames and the rounds it was carrying were cooking off. The Ontos' white phosphorous rounds were exploding and producing thick billows of white smoke, as well as deadly flaming phosphorous, which was arcing from the Ontos like fireworks on the Fourth of July.

Our ammo carrier Hathaway was trying to provide belts of ammo for our gun the best he could. Many of the riflemen in our squad had been assigned extra belts of ammo to carry for the machine gun. Hathaway was crawling from one Marine to another collecting the belts of ammo. He would then make his way back to the gun and hand me the ammo. We had run out of ammo and Hathaway had not returned to re-supply us. I began searching for him and finally found him sitting on the ground with his back resting on a small bush. What the hell was he doing? He would get killed sitting up like that. I screamed at him, "Get down before you get killed and get us some more ammo."

He slowly went to the prone position. He looked at me with eyes that were vacant and hopeless and said, "There isn't any more ammo."

I hadn't fired my rifle very much because I was busy feeding the machine gun but now there was no reason why I couldn't. I began loading clip after clip into my M-16 rifle and firing bursts into the enemy tree line. Glock was only armed with a 45-caliber handgun. He drew it from his holster and fired several rounds. It sounded like a kid's cap gun in comparison to all the weapons that were firing around at us. I turned and looked at Glock as he turned to look at me. We both had a wry smile on our faces and knew firing that cap shooter was useless. Glock dropped the handgun and said, 'I'm going to get a real weapon I'll be right back.' There was military equipment strewn all over the battle field dropped there by dead and wounded Marines so it wouldn't be too hard to come up with a rifle for Glock.[59]

Foxtrot and the Alpha command group, with Figard, were skirmishing with their foe at an extremely close range, ten to fifteen meters, in exactly the area where Echo and its five tanks had already passed through.[60] This shows how well camouflaged and disciplined the North Vietnamese were. The enemy sat and waited as Echo passed over them and held their fire until Foxtrot was almost on top of them. This action took place about 400 yards behind and to the right of Echo.[61] The most brutal fire came from east of the village of Phu Oc, about 2,000 meters east of Con Thien.[62] The action was so serious that Echo Company had to remain stationary for the remainder of the afternoon.[63]

"As we moved out," Mitchell said, "you could see the jets bombing the hills ahead. Artillery was passing over from Camp Carrol and Dong Ha. On our left, we saw a UH-34 Med-evac helicopter get shot down. We found out later the crew was rescued. The further north we went the more fighting we heard."[64]

The fire support Mitchell reported was at 1230H and was in response to Foxtrot being bushwhacked.[65] The artillery bombardment and air strikes lasted four hours.[66]

Dallape remembered the fire support coming in:

Air support finally began to arrive. Huey helicopter gun ships circled overhead peppering the woods with their machine guns and swooping in to unload pods of rockets into the enemy line of fire. I could only catch a glimpse of them as they dove into position to fire their rockets and quickly climbed out of sight. Then we heard a high-pitched roar of a jet's engines flying overhead. It was a Phantom jet circling over our position. It banked sharply to the right and then began to dive. The engine sounds peaked as it roared over our heads. I could see its Navy blue belly as it passed directly over us heading for the village that was hidden behind the tree line in front of us. It must have been the outlying part of the village that we had just passed through. How long ago had that been? Was it an hour ago, several hours ago or had it been just a few minutes? Time meant nothing. The battle seemed to go on forever, yet there was no comprehension of anything that had happened in the past or any thought of the future. We were suspended in time and place. The only thing that mattered was what was happening right then. I learned later that the village to the front of us was filled with NVA troops and equipment rushing in to support their comrades in the tree line. As the jet reached its lowest ebb over the village, I could hear 50-caliber machine gun batteries firing fusillade after fusillade at the Phantom jet. The jet would release its payload of bombs and climb straight up into the sky. The sound of its deafening jet engines and the blast of the impacting bombs took your breath away. I could feel the pressure of the explosion impacting on my chest. Again and again Phantom after Phantom would unleash its cargo of death. Every time they dove in the kill, we would flatten ourselves as close to the ground as we could. There were times that I felt as thin as a piece of paper and wished that I had the digging ability of the lowly worm.[67]

Trying to coordinate aircraft, artillery, medical evacuation and resupply turned out to be extremely difficult. Resupply and Medevacs continually interfered with planes and fire support, and jets interfered with gunfire. When resupply or hospital flights arrived, supporting fire had to be stopped, and when air came in, artillery fire had to be checked. This resulted, observers said, in good targets being lost.[68] Oots complained that on one occasion he had to wait five hours for artillery support.[69] Landers and Fulford were also unhappy with the confusion.[70] The optimum situation would be for all these elements to work together smoothly. Unfortunately, when a conflict developed, a choice had to be made.

The argument here was between mission and men. Which should take priority? Do those in command resupply their men and take care of their wounded, or do they destroy the enemy? This is an issue of continual debate in the military. Some professionals maintain the mission must be given preference. The commander must first accomplish his task, they say. Other experts counter that the men's welfare is of utmost importance. They point out that, an officer cannot accomplish his objective without his men. This topic continues to fuel discussion within our military leadership. Among the grunts there wasn't any doubt about what should be done. Their goal was survival.

There were also problems with resupply. Combat service support personnel were not issued a copy of the Operation Order and were not aware of the battle they were supposed to support.[71] Emergency resupply was also hindered by the intensity of the fighting, and it proved to be almost impossible to get supplies to 2/26. Lastly, there were problems at the ammunition supply point. The Marines in charge didn't know what was available, and even though this was an emergency situation, some acted with indifference. Consequently, three days went by before 2/26 was able to get additional 60mm mortar and M-79 grenade launcher ammunition.[72]

The ferocious casualties inflicted on 2/26 overwhelmed the Dong Ha medical facilities. The medical personnel were praised for their efforts in a difficult situation, but the morgue was not large enough to accommodate all of the corpses. The Medevac helicopter pilots, as always, earned accolades from the grunts for their extreme bravery under fire.[73] While the rear area was trying to sort itself out, an attempt to save Foxtrot was about to start.

News of Foxtrot's situation filtered back to the grunts of Golf.

"We got the word" that Foxtrot had made heavy contact, Mitchell recalled, "this was around 1400H. The message was passed to stop and eat, as it may be a while before we get to eat again."[74]

Golf Company was ordered forward, fifteen minutes later,[75] to break through to Foxtrot and reconnect the column. The rear platoon of Foxtrot, Curly's 1st Platoon, was surrounded.[76] As the Marines moved down the wide dirt path, they could hear the church bell ringing and could see the civilians running in the opposite direction.[77]

As Golf moved forward, Mitchell "noticed 81's digging in on our right. As we approached them we came under intense automatic weapons fire."[78]

Cauble, a New York transplant to California, remembered the sudden enormous volume of shooting to the front.

"Maybe," said Pfc. Danny Higgins, "they are just reconning by fire."

Everyone else knew the shooting was too hot for it to be spoiling fire (Troops would sporadically discharge their weapons as they advanced. This was done to flush out the enemy).

The Marines then received the whispered order: "Fix bayonets and stand by for action!"

They had been given a primeval call to battle. This command shocked everyone into the reality of the situation. The moment had come. They were about to march into hell. From now on the grunts would live moment to moment. The sights, sounds and smells burned into their minds forever. Decades would not dull the horror.[79]

Golf Company, recalled Mitchell, "quickly got on line and assaulted the hedgerows to our front. There was a field between the road we were on and the hedgerow the NVA were in."

There were seventy yards of open ground to cross.[80] 1st Platoon pushed down the road. 1st Squad was on the path, 2nd Squad was to the left and 3rd Squad was to the right. 2nd Platoon swung off the road to the right of 1st Platoon. 3rd Platoon was held in reserve.[81]

"The call for guns went out," Mitchell said, "so we moved up to within fifteen yards of the hedgerow. We were then called back by Sgt. Perez because he didn't want the machine gun knocked out of action."[82]

Perez, a former boxer, was the platoon sergeant and an extremely tough individual.[83]

"We moved back about twenty yards and set up," recalled Mitchell.

Moments later, the spot where Mitchell's gun team had been, received a direct hit from an 57mm recoilless rifle. Then the entire NVA position in the hedgerow opened fire.

Mitchell remembered, "Rounds were flying everywhere. Lance Cpl. Whilton A. McCarthy of Charlotte North Carolina was killed by the 57mm round. Also hit was Lance Cpl. Shurtz. He was shot in the side. A corpsman took his M-16 when he was medevaced."

The Marines couldn't break through the enemy position and were pinned down by the vicious fire.[84] Being under fire was a terrifying experience. The men felt frightened, panic-stricken and trapped. While their Marine training quickly asserted itself and they were able to endure the torment, they would forever be haunted by nightmares of what they went through.[85]

Moving cautiously down the road was 1st Squad, 1st Platoon. As the men advanced down the path, they took withering fire and were shooting enemy snipers out of the trees.[86] To the left, 2nd Squad made no contact and moved into a reserve position behind the berm.[87] Within seconds, Richard Ross recalled, 1st Squad, which started with thirteen men, had only four men left.[88]

Golf Company regrouped and with astonishing grit, again assaulted the NVA position.

F-4 Phantom (*USNI*)

Mitchell wrote,

an Ontos was moved up ten yards to our left. We were going to use it against the hedgerow. As the gunner in the turret started to fire the 30-caliber machine gun, a B-40 rocket (RPG) scored a direct hit. I saw his tanker helmet blow about ten feet into the air. I don't know if his head was still in it or not. All three crew members were killed and Marines around it were wounded. We had to withdraw back to the road. We had some protection there, as there was a five-foot stone wall between the road and the field we were in.[89]

Lying down behind the berm with 2nd Squad, Cauble remembered seeing the runner for 1st Platoon, Lance Cpl. Dennis Maben, running all over the battlefield carrying messages. Maben was of average height and weight, and always seemed to wear a mischievous smile. Eventually, Maben became so exhausted, Cauble saw him just walking up and down the road. Later that afternoon, he was shot in the stomach and was sent to the rear.[90]

Yet another valiant attempt by Golf to cross the field was driven back by fierce enemy resistance. The Marines returned to the protection of the stone wall.

"You could hear the rounds flying overhead," said Mitchell. "It sounded like a bunch of bees flying past."[91]

The company was unable to move. Captain Oots walked to the front of the command. Everyone else was lying down but Oots was in the open, standing tall with rounds scattering around him.

Oots looked around and yelled, "Come on, let's get 'em."

He then led Golf, bayonets at the ready and jaws set, in another attack on the NVA position. Oots was recommended for the Silver Star.[92]

"This time we meant to get them," wrote Mitchell, "We got on line for the assault. Our machine gun set up in one corner of the field to cover the rifle squads."[93]

Cpl. Wright's fire team from 3rd Squad received orders to attack an NVA strongpoint and they dropped their excess gear before the assault.[94] Wright then led his fire team against the hedgerow. They reduced the enemy position with grenades and small arms fire. Wright was recommended for the Silver Star.[95]

pinned down. Crowe emptied his 45 at the NVA in the hole." A grunt "threw a grenade and forced the NVA to close the lid."

With the Marines on top of them, the North Vietnamese decided to abandon their position.

"About this time, everything broke loose," Mitchell said. Rounds were flying everywhere and Mitchell and his gun crew took cover. "I remember seeing some ants on the ground, and thinking how lucky they were, because nobody could see them and try to kill them. About this time Fields started yelling that I had been hit. I was feeling all over trying to find out where, when Bannister said it had hit my e-tool cover. The round then hit the ground between Bannister and me. I never heard or felt a thing."

The round missed Mitchell's neck by only two inches.[96]

The assistant radioman for Golf, Cpl. James W. Hart, Jr., defiantly ran out into the open to provide covering fire for the assault on the enemy position. An enemy shell exploded near him, wounding him in the leg. Despite his wound, Hart then advanced on the hedgerow, leading the attack. He reached a point close to the enemy entrenchment and delivered point-blank fire. An enemy round went through his helmet and caused a serious head wound. Hart took no notice of the pain and the blood pouring from his wounds, and continued to fire into the enemy rampart. Meanwhile, other Americans assaulted and destroyed the NVA emplacement. Hart was awarded the Silver Star.[97] While Hart's wounds were being treated by several corpsmen, Cauble recalled him standing there, covered in blood, mad as hell, swearing and screaming to get back into the fight.[98]

Off to the right of 1st Platoon, 2nd Platoon was also taking the offense. As Cpl. Richard E. Moffit maneuvered his squad toward an enemy hedgerow, they came under blistering machine-gun fire. Moffit's squad was trapped by the fire. With unbelievable courage Moffit single-handedly attacked the enemy bunker. He jumped into the NVA bastion and killed all of its occupants. Moffit was awarded the Navy Cross for the heroism he displayed on May 16 and May 17.[99]

The communists finally broke and ran for their lives, leaving behind a few men as a rear guard.[100] A Leatherneck with an M-79 grenade launcher hit a fleeing enemy soldier in the back at 100 yards, turning him into a red blur.[101]

Richard Ross on right (*Brown Collection*)

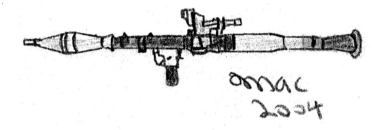

NVA RPG-7V

Dennis Maben on left, author on right (*Author's Collection*)

While Mitchell was taking a drink from his canteen, two enemy soldiers jumped up and started running away. "Fields grabbed the M-60 and opened fire," and the rest of the squad joined in. "No way we could have missed them." Artillery then started mowing down the communists as they ran back.[102]

The men of Golf, proving their mettle, finally broke through to Foxtrot. Dallape remembered the moment:

> "The enemy fire from the tree line began to die down. The air strikes must have broken their line of defense. We were still receiving sporadic rounds when Golf Company began to arrive. I approached the first machine gun team, I saw and asked them for ammo for our guns. The machine gunner from Golf handed me one hundred rounds of belted ammo. We were back in business again."[103]

Mitchell believed Fields was the Marine who gave Dallape ammunition. "I think that was Jesse Fields who gave the F Co. gunner ammo on May 16. I remember him giving someone ammo that day."[104]

When the men of Golf got to the point at which Foxtrot had been surprised, they saw the horrible sight of lifeless Americans sprawled all over the road. The surviving men from Foxtrot that Cauble saw were drenched in sweat, exhausted and in a state of shock.[105]

The terror of combat proved too much for one Leatherneck. Mitchell saw him in his foxhole crying. He refused to come out of his hole. The corpsmen later medevaced him, even though he wasn't wounded. For the rest of his tour in Vietnam the crying Marine was shunned by his comrades.[106]

The numerous casualties of 2/26 had to be transported to the rear. Golf's executive officer, twenty-three-year-old Brown, organized the removal of the wounded to safety. This was done while under fire from the NVA rear guard. Brown repeatedly exposed himself to fire, while personally moving wounded Americans. He located an enemy position only twenty meters away and led five men from Golf's command group in an attack.[107] Three of the five Leathernecks were injured in the attack, including Brown, who received an AK-47 round in the neck.[108] Although wounded, Brown continued to direct the attack.[109] The NVA dugout was finally destroyed by a 90mm round from a tank. Brown received the Bronze Star.[110]

Operation Hickory—Martinez (*Brown Collection*)

Also assisting the casualties was Mitchell. "I helped carry two of the wounded to the Medevac helicopter. One guy had his left arm hanging on by a thread."

The other Marine was missing three fingers from his right hand and had been hit in the face by shrapnel.[111] Curly assisted in the movement of Foxtrot's injured[112] and Gunnery Sgt. Donalano Francisco Martinez, while being shot at, helped organize and supported the evacuation of thirty-one wounded.[113] The hurt grunts were taking fire as they were being sent back.

Fulford recalled,

> After we took the mortaring on the 16th, I remember vividly a fellow sitting on a tank, smoking a cigarette very calmly, and…both his legs were missing from the knee down. …On another vehicle, another wounded fellow was reclining, waiting to be medevaced, the mortars started back up again. One explosion took the top of his head off, and his brain matter was spread all over.[114]

Carrying the corpses of their buddies was gut-wrenching and heart-breaking. Men sobbed as they moved the dead. Smelling, tasting, and touching death was not something they would soon forget and would disturb their sleep for many years to come.[115]

There were so many hurt that there were not enough helicopters to take them all out and enemy fire made it impossible for the copters to land nearby. Many injured Leathernecks were put on tanks and Ontos, and taken to a secure area. There they were loaded onto helicopters or trucks to be driven or flown back to the Battalion Aid Station in Dong Ha.[116] The corpsmen moved into the Catholic Church and turned it into a hospital.[117] Some U.S. troops refused to be medevaced—Brown, for example—and there were a lot of walking wounded who did not seek treatment.[118]

Oots believed that the aggressive attack by Golf, literally hopping into the enemy fortifications to kill them, was responsible for breaking up the enemy ambush and rescuing Foxtrot.[119]

After Foxtrot was relieved, the battalion withdrew to just inside the southern boundary of the firebreak.[120] Before 2/26 retreated, Marine riflemen advanced as far forward as possible and threw red smoke grenades to mark NVA positions for air strikes.[121] The battle had lasted four hours.

"That was one of the hellishest firefights I've ever been in in my life," said Giordano. "They pinned us down. I looked at my watch, and I remember it was exactly 1200H on the 16th, and this went on right up till 1600H. We had fire coming in all afternoon. They just tore us up bad. It's shameful to say, but there was nothing we could do. It was four hours of pure hell."[122]

Before the grunts fell back, they had to recover their dead. Near the road, J. C. Christian, a tall, thin Marine, was looking for McCarthy and had to be physically restrained until the Americans could move forward in force. When McCarthy's body was finally found it had been booby-trapped by the North Vietnamese. A grenade was lodged between McCarthy's legs. 1st Platoon's Commanding Officer, 2nd Lt. Gerst, wanted to set off the booby-trap before recovering the body.

"Nobody agreed with this and the grenade was removed," wrote Mitchell, and the body was carried back.[123]

The battalion set its fieldworks around the Catholic Church.[124]

"I remember," said Mitchell, "watching them bring out the bodies of dead and wounded Marines and it seemed like it would never end. Our battalion had lost a lot of good men."[125]

Hotel Company arrived after the fight was over.

Hancock wrote, "As we got inside the perimeter, there was a line of dead Marines lying under ponchos along the road… it was a long line."[126]

The day's toll was not yet complete.

Everyone started building earthworks as soon as the perimeter was set. About fifteen minutes after Alpha command group arrived near Echo, with what was left of Foxtrot, incoming mortar rounds started raining down on Echo's position. Echo Company lost two killed and eight to ten wounded.[127]

Hancock has a detailed memory of what happened to Hotel after it arrived:

> A man named Whitt (not sure of the spelling) and myself were positioned in the middle of a large dried-out rice paddy. We dropped our gear and dug a hole. The ground was hard and we were tired so our hole was about six feet

long, two and a half feet wide, and about eighteen inches deep. It wasn't a good fighting hole. When we were done, I went to the position next to us (about fifty yards away) to see what they were doing. Their hole was along the rice paddie dike and there was a tree line on the dike. One of the guys and I sat down with our backs to the dike and started talking about what went on. Then I saw the guy jerk, and I heard a crack. A sniper had shot him in the knee. The other guy and I dragged him into their hole and called for the corpsman. We tried to stop the bleeding as much as we could and the corpsman was there almost immediately and took over. There were no more shots. I went back to my hole.[128]

Golf set up near the Catholic Church. The church had a well and a few Marines were able to fill their canteens.

"Every now and then an NVA sniper would fire a shot, but he never hit anyone," remembered Mitchell.[129]

During the night Golf was probed by several groups of two to three of the enemy. At 0530H two NVA soldiers were spotted walking down the road by a machine-gun team. The Americans waited until they were within six feet before they opened fire. Both men were cut down.[130]

That same night Hotel was mortared. Hancock told what happened:

That evening as it got dark, four Ontos pulled-in about twenty-five yards behind our hole. We thought this was great; we had all this firepower behind us, and they could help us keep watch. Sometime later (it wasn't midnight yet because we were still on 100 percent watch) we heard mortar rounds dropping into tubes, a lot of them. At first we thought they were ours, they sounded really close, then we heard the whistle of the incoming rounds. They were trying to hit the Ontos. Rounds started hitting all around us. Whitt and I got down in our hole as best as we could. The men from the Ontos must have been sleeping on the ground because immediately we heard the screaming and the call for the corpsmen. The corpsmen never hesitated; we could hear them yelling that they were coming and running right through the mortar barrage. They took care of those men while the rounds were falling all around them. The rounds hit in our area for what seemed like five minutes. Then they started walking the rounds down our perimeter. Whitt and I got up and got ready for the ground attack we were sure was coming following the mortars. It never came. We could still hear the rounds falling somewhere down on the perimeter and were talking about how stupid we had been to dig such a large hole, when the rounds started walking back toward our position. When they got back to where we were, they really hit us hard again. We could once again hear men being hit. Then our counter-fire started and their mortars stopped. There were men hit all up and down the lines. We tried to bring in Medevac choppers, but every time one got close, the NVA opened up on it. I'm not sure if they got the wounded out that night. The officers and NCOs came around and checked the holes. We had so many men hit that they had to reset the perimeter and make it smaller. They sent another man, Robert Ramirez, to join Whitt and me in our position, I guess because we were so exposed out in the rice paddie. We dug a better fighting hole.[131]

Ross L. Webster of Hotel also recalled the bombardment: "I remember sitting up that night in our foxholes and I could hear the gooks dropping the mortars in the tubes prior to the mortars hitting in and around our foxholes. It seemed as though you could reach out and shake hands with them."[132]

One American couldn't stand the strain of the bombardment, wrote Californian Roger Chicoine, "He went crazy and tried to get up and was flown out the next day."[133]

Many U.S. troops suspected the accuracy of the enemy mortars was due to a spotter who had a radio and was inside of the battalion's perimeter.[134] Jets were called in and they plastered the communist mortars with seventy-five radar-controlled strikes.[135]

United Press International Photographer Frank Johnson entered the Catholic Church, and watched as a friend of his, a wounded USMC combat correspondent, died before his eyes.

Elsewhere, "A Marine moaned, 'Water, somebody please give me some water. I'm going to pass out,'" Johnson said. "I looked around. Most of the Leathernecks were almost out of water. I opened my canteen, leaned back and poured some over his head."[136]

Left to right: Christian, Long (*Mitchell Collection*)

Operation Hickory—"That day we got hit hard, so the hole was dug deep for the night."–Brown (*Brown Collection*)

Operation Hickory—North Vietnamese soldier (*Brown Collection*)

Ron Marmon and Roger Chicoine (*Chicoine Collection*)

The end of May 16 found 2/26 decimated. The "butcher's bill" totaled fifteen dead and sixty injured. The Marines counted seventy-nine North Vietnamese bodies.[137]

The Marine Corps was having a hard time getting its wounded and dead out, and the men were running out of ammunition. Everyone was thirsty, and few could sleep. Over the next three days they would be living off the adrenalin rush from combat. The grunts waited anxiously for morning to come.[138]

3

"Much Bravery Shown Today"

May 17

BACK HOME, unknown to the men of 2/26, they were big news. The front page of *The New York Times* reported that a Marine company had been thrown back "with heavy losses"[1] and *Time* magazine had a feature article on the battle in its May 26 issue.[2] The grunts would have been surprised by all the attention.

At dawn on May 17, Hancock found out how lucky he had been the night before:

> The next morning when daylight came we looked and six mortar rounds had landed within six feet of our hole. The packs we had left outside the hole were blown to pieces. We laughed and joked, but it was that nervous laughter that Marines do when they know they were lucky to get through the night.[3]

Golf and Hotel moved out at 0800H to join Echo and Foxtrot near the firebreak.[4] At noon the Marines halted and were given a canteen of water each. They were told the one canteen would have to last until the next day.[5] The battalion was re-supplied with ammunition, although there was still a shortage of 60mm mortar and M-79 grenade launcher rounds.[6] Enemy fire was still interfering with supply and medical evacuation.[7]

The battalion proceeded toward the firebreak four hours later.[8] Figard had 2/26 lined-up for a textbook frontal assault, with Golf on the left and Echo on the right.[9] Foxtrot was on the path, with the Alpha command group, behind Golf and Echo. Hotel was 300 meters to the rear of Foxtrot and the command group.[10] Golf had two tanks[11] and Echo had five.[12]

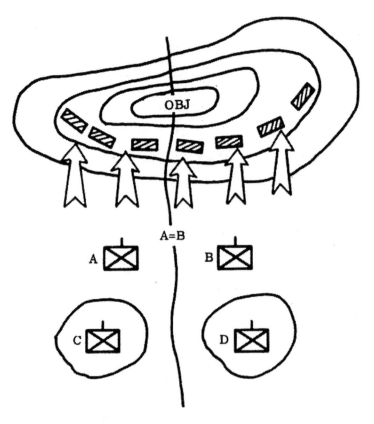

USMC–Frontal attack (*USMC*)

Both companies had their armor up front and each company had a frontage of 100-150 yards.[13] 2nd Platoon led Golf forward, with 1st and 3rd Platoon, echeloned behind.[14]

As 1st Platoon started its onslaught, eighteen-year-old Cauble remembered seeing a corpsman visibly shaking with fear, holding a cigarette, and talking to the Golf command group. He must have had a premonition, because he was killed later that day.[15]

Golf and Echo were using the road as a boundary. Golf had one of its tanks on Echo's side and when the tracked vehicle crossed over to rejoin Golf, it drove onto a mine. A huge explosion shook and damaged the armored behemoth, putting it out of action.[16] As the lead elements of Golf and Echo got halfway across the firebreak, they started receiving artillery and mortar fire on the tree line directly to their front.[17] At the time, Cauble thought this was friendly supporting fire.[18] Just as the grunts had fearlessly advanced to a point where they would have started taking casualties, the enemy fire stopped.[19] As Golf entered the tree line they saw about thirty NVA soldiers milling around in a state of confusion.[20] The tank with Golf fired three canister rounds (which were similar to large shotgun shells)[21] into them, taking out several of the enemy.[22] The rest of the North Vietnamese fled.[23] The two companies continued their offense and suddenly came under violent fire from the front and flanks.[24] The battalion was moving right into the NVA defensive U.[25] The "confused" soldiers that Golf encountered may have been bait to draw the Leathernecks into their defensive fire zones.[26] Echo and Golf probably swung another platoon to the front and kept their 3rd Platoon in reserve. The two companies' frontage was now almost 400 meters.[27] Golf's 1st Platoon was in all likelihood to the left of 2nd Platoon, and 3rd Platoon was in reserve.[28] Both companies received concentrated machine gun and semi- and full-automatic small arms fire. The NVA fired RPGs and recoilless rifles directly into the Marines' front ranks[29] and enemy mortar and artillery fire was precisely placed onto the assaulting Americans.

The grunts had thrusted 300 yards from the firebreak when they encountered this accurate fire.[30] Golf was hit by two artillery shells containing tear gas. This caused some temporary confusion because the men were not carrying gas masks. The fumes quickly dissipated and the attack continued.[31] By aggressively moving forward about 100 meters, Golf and Echo were able to disrupt the North Vietnamese defensive fire plan. The U.S. troops, instead of taking cover, moved beyond the point where the enemy had registered their weapons. Consequently, the NVA's mortar and artillery barrage ceased.[32] The enemy soldiers stubbornly refused to leave their positions and had to be blown out. Echo was able to smash the enemy defenses with the guns of its five tanks. The NVA repeatedly tried to knock out the Marine armor with RPGs. The enemy would close to within 30 meters of an armored vehicle before they would fire. Even at this range, either their marksmanship or their weapon was faulty. After numerous attempts, the NVA still only managed to hit one Leatherneck vehicle.[33] Golf, with only one tank left, had to depend on its grunts to overrun the enemy positions.

As Golf's 1st Platoon advanced it was peppered by small arms and mortar fire. The U.S. troops were firing as they assaulted the enemy positions, so they didn't realize they were being shot at until men started dropping. The Leathernecks were caught in an open meadow. Three Marines were wounded and 1st Platoon retired. The platoon reorganized, and with remarkable pluck, again lunged forward.

"I was in the middle of the field when everything broke loose," wrote Mitchell. "A row of banana trees to my right was cut down by bullets. It looked like a giant knife leveled them with one swoop. I saw a rifle grenade come from my right and hit one of our guys to my left. It hit him in the leg, but failed to explode."

The platoon took cover and could not move. Ignoring the danger, Brown, the company's executive officer and former commander of 1st Platoon, came up and said, "Let's go get 'em."

The platoon, revealing its élan, again charged the enemy. The NVA defense had a 7.62mm machine gun on wheels, with a shield for protection and was manned by a three-man crew. On either side of the machine gun were infantry in spider holes. 1st and 3rd Squads hit the right side of the enemy and engaged in a point-blank firefight.[34]

Perez, by himself, took out the machine gun's protective force on the right and was recommended for the Silver Star.[35] On the left, 2nd Squad walked up to the North Vietnamese defenses. The enemy soldiers were so preoccupied with the rest of the Marine platoon; they didn't notice this new threat. 2nd Squad was standing right next to the hedgerow, when the NVA finally opened up. All the Marines could see was the bushes shaking, muzzle flashes, smoke from weapons and numerous grenades flying through the air towards them. The action was fast and furious. Seconds seemed to stretch into hours. The fighting, though, only lasted a few minutes. The enemy promptly started to turn their machine gun around to shoot at 2nd Squad. Fortune smiled on the squad and the enemy gun crew was eliminated before it could start spewing death. Twenty-year-old Lance Cpl. Warren J. Noonan, a tall, strongly built redhead, and Pfc Brunton, nicknamed "Bulldog" because he was short and stocky, were caught in the open. The rest of the squad took cover. The two grunts fought it out toe-to-toe with the enemy. Both were wounded numerous times, but kept on shooting. Luckily, few of the enemy grenades actually exploded. One stick-handled grenade struck Brunton in the chest, bounced off and failed to discharge. Cauble's fire team leader attempted to flank the enemy by moving his men through the hedgerow on the left. The foliage proved to be too thick and the Marines were unable to get near the enemy entrenchment. The fire team quickly rejoined the battle going on in front of the hedgerow. Squad Leader Cpl. Lyons, who everyone called "Bones" because he was tall and thin as a rail, stepped forward firing at the enemy and tossing a white phosphorous grenade into their rampart.[36] His explosive found its mark and the NVA security on the left side of the position were put out of commission.[37]

As Lyons pulled back to reload, Cauble advanced, yelled, "Grenade!" and threw a fragmentation bomb into the enemy's nest. Everyone ducked down. The earth heaved and the air around them was sucked away by the force of the detonation. The dull thud of the report made their ears ache. Cauble then moved up next to the hedgerow and fired a full magazine indiscriminately into the enemy.[38] 1st Platoon was ordered back. Golf's tank was brought up and it "raked the hedgerow."[39] After this the enemy fire ceased.[40] The North Vietnamese had abandoned their defenses and retreated, leaving behind their dead.

Warren J. Noonan, far right (*Author's Collection*)

Brunton (*Author's Collection*)

Operation Hickory—NVA stick-handled grenades
(*Brown Collection*)

Oots observed thirty-five to forty NVA soldiers running across his front to the northeast. According to Oots, the North Vietnamese, when confronted with aggressive troops, broke. If cornered, they would fight until you killed them. However, if they had a chance to get away, they would take it.[41]

Furiously, 1st Platoon again sortied.[42] 1st and 3rd Squads came up to the enemy's position, and found three dead North Vietnamese in one fortification and another three NVA corpses in a second hole. An enemy soldier jumped up suddenly, immediately in front of Mitchell and tried to say something. Next to Mitchell was Christian and he fired an entire magazine into the enemy soldier's head and chest.[43] The men's "blood was up" and they were in foul moods. War is a brutal business. Noonan and Brunton were recommended for Bronze Stars and Lyons was cited for a Silver Star.[44]

2nd Platoon, in the interim, was having its own difficulties. It ran into a hail of small arms fire and artillery and mortar shells showered on top of it. Two Marines were killed and eleven were hurt, forcing the platoon to take cover.[45] Undaunted, Moffit assaulted an enemy machine gun nest and destroyed it, single handedly, with grenades and small arms fire.[46] For this action and his previous day's exploits, Moffit was awarded the Navy Cross.[47] Platoon Commander, 2nd Lt. Daniel R. Phipps, took charge of one of his cornered squads. He directed their fire against an enemy bunker and was hit in the back by an exploding enemy grenade. Nevertheless, Phipps continued in action and the enemy force soon fled their dugout. Phipps then put together a pursuit of the North Vietnamese and again the Marines came under destructive fire. Resolutely, Phipps again led his men against this new NVA bastion and forced the enemy to flee. Once more he was wounded. Phipps refused to be medevaced and stayed with his men so he could make sure they consolidated their position.[48] For his courage, he was given the Silver Star.

While Golf and Echo were battling at the front, the enemy started mortaring the battalion command post. The point where the road intersected the firebreak turned out to be a good aiming point for the enemy and they seemed to be on target with the very first round they fired.[49] Forty-four 82-mm mortar rounds hit the Alpha command group around 1600H, injuring Figard and nineteen other Marines.[50]

Wickersham wrote:

> As we were already "saddled-up," I had all my gear on and with my radio on my back (I provided communication for our 81mm mortars and was attached to the battalion command group) and my feet dangling in someone's foxhole from the night before, I watched the battalion commander and about fifteen other people gathered around having a meeting before we moved out for the day. They were about fifteen yards from me when the first incoming mortar landed right in the middle of the group. It landed right at the feet of Cpl. Gene Lillie, the battalion commanders' radioman. He lost a leg immediately and the corpsmen got to the group and helped everyone. In the meantime, our 81mm mortars, with incoming dropping all around us, started to return fire. After the incoming stopped, the wounded were placed on an Ontos and I went to speak to Gene, but he was so shot full of morphine that he didn't know I was talking to him.[51]

Fosmo recalled,

> All but one radio operator lost arms or legs...one was still trying to transmit after losing both legs and having the back of the radio blown open.[52] The radio operator who didn't get wounded was named Sorenson. Sorenson was in shock for a couple of days and didn't talk or know what was going on. The doctor said to keep him with us so he was with someone he knew. When he came out of it he didn't remember anything after the mortar round hit.[53]

The battalion was strongly committed to the front and enemy fire was arcing around both flanks. There was also considerable confusion caused by the destruction of the Alpha command group. Fulford said, "we decided it was best to stop and regroup before moving forward again. I called for another unit to move up on my right flank."[54]

Fulford may have saved the command. The North Vietnamese, unexpectedly, did not press the attack once the Marines stopped their sally. Most likely, they were rigidly adhering to their plan and saw no reason to stick their necks out. The enemy was content to let the Americans knock their heads against prepared positions. That afternoon, the Leathernecks didn't need any encouragement to dig in. Echo stayed on the right and Golf was on the left. The grunts put the tanks on the front lines and dug their foxholes around them.[55]

There were many dead North Vietnamese within the Marines' perimeter and, the platoon diary said, "had to bury gooks, they stunk so bad."[56] The sickly sweet smell of rotting flesh hung over the battlefield.[57] Two hours later the command post was mortared again, this time with thirty-five 82mm mortar rounds. The grunts lost six more wounded.[58] The men of 2/26 concentrated on evacuating their casualties and bringing in resupply, but their efforts were again hampered by the pitiless enemy fire. The helicopters couldn't land, so they dropped supplies to the Marines as they flew over. The ammunition and food landed in good shape, but the water containers exploded on contact. Without water the food became inedible. The grunts were reduced to taking water from dead and wounded Leathernecks. They even tried to drink from captured NVA canteens, but found they contained an undrinkable syrupy tea.[59] Gunnery Sergeant Martinez again distinguished himself by moving twenty disabled Marines to safety while under fire.[60]

Due to the peril facing 2/26, Lt. Col. John J. Peeler's 2nd Battalion, 9th Marines was diverted from another mission, and received orders to follow 2/26's route and then to move forward onto 2/26's right flank.[61] John Murphy remembered the march:

> I was with H 2/9 securing and patrolling Highway 1 ('the street without joy') and the mountains around lower Quang Tri Province when we were sent to Dong Ha 16 May, and immediately to 'Leatherneck Square' (The area south of the DMZ with the following outposts as its corners: Con Thien (NW), Cam Lo Hill (SW), Cua Viet (SE) and Gia Linh (NE).[62]). On 17 May, we headed north. As we approached a church located on a simple road/path, I could see evidence of what was a fierce engagement. On the trail were NVA bodies.[63]

Brunton above, author on left, "Bones" in center
(*Author's Collection*)

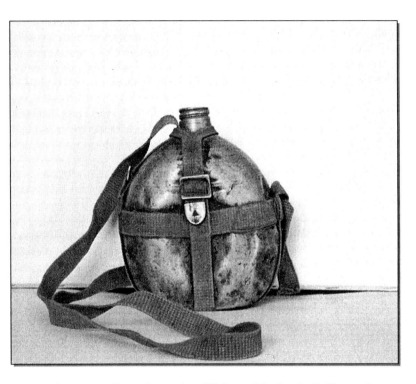

NVA canteen from Operation Hickory (*Author's Collection*)

It was as if they were following a wounded animal.

Peeler's battalion spent May 17 following 2/26's bloody trail and by 1600H the next day they were in position on 2/26's right.[64] Lt. Col. James S. Wilson's 3rd Battalion, 9th Marines was directed to cover the left, or western, flank of 2/26.[65] Lt. Col. William J. Masterpool was sent by the 3rd Marine Division to replace Figard as battalion commander. He had just completed his command of 3rd Battalion, 4th Marines and had joined the division staff.[66] Masterpool was a veteran officer with a dry sense of humor.[67]

That night the Marines put out listening posts and the enemy tested 2/26's perimeter. Golf Company at 2045H observed two NVA soldiers walking down the road, one carried a tripod for a 57mm recoilless rifle and the other had an 82mm mortar round. Both were killed by a shotgun blast from a Golf Company squad leader.[68] The enemy hammered the command post with about two-hundred 82mm mortar rounds three hours later. This bombardment wounded thirteen grunts.[69] The Leathernecks could hear the NVA mortar tubes firing. There were so many shooting that it sounded like a machine gun. Mortars make a very distinctive hollow "whomp" sound when they fire and are a high-angle weapon. The Americans could hear them fire, the rounds would be in the air, and the men would know they were coming down. All the grunts could do was take cover and hope the shells didn't land on their heads. The Marines spent another sleepless night. The talk was that 2/26 was surrounded, but help was on the way.[70]

The platoon diary of May 17 said, "much bravery shown today."[71] Destroying those who wish to kill your comrades is an entirely reasonable course of action. However, the natural reaction to being shot at is to run away or take cover. Commanders realized either option would place their people in greater danger than advancing to kill the enemy. If the men turned tail, their backs would make an easy target for their opponent because no one would be firing back at them. Of course, there are times when a unit will be forced back. On these occasions, the men must retire slowly and carefully, with covering fire to protect them as they go. On the other hand, if troops try to hunker down, the enemy would be able to zero in on their location. Circumstances can force a unit to stand on the defensive. It then becomes a simple object for enemy mortars and artillery. People need to be trained and disciplined to overcome their instinctual fear and when well led, they will move forward under fire. Only a small number will advance on their own initiative. These few we call heroes.

The day ended with two Marines killed and seventy-seven injured. The Leathernecks accounted for fourteen dead North Vietnamese.[72] By this point the Americans had stopped reporting minor wounds. Many corpsmen had been lost in the fighting and the few that were left, were overwhelmed by the sheer number of seriously hurt Marines.

There were exceptions. Cauble stumbled out of the bush with his arms bleeding from flying metal fragments. A corpsman just happened to be standing nearby. He said, "Oh, another purple heart" and wrote Cauble's name down.

With fewer and fewer medical personnel available, the Marine officers drafted riflemen to take the place of the lost corpsmen. Without any training, they did as well as could be expected.[73] The battalion had lost more than fifteen percent of its men and was frantically short of water. Prairie IV was ending and a rescue mission was about to begin.

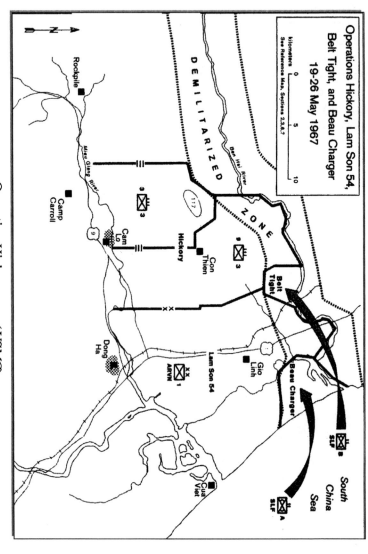

Operation Hickory map (USMC)

4

"Helpless Under the Mortar Fire"

May 18

OPERATION HICKORY, said the official Marine Corps history, began on May 18, 1967.[1] The Command Chronology of 2/26, however, listed the start of the operation as 1700H May 17.[2] There is another anomaly with the Marine Corps' history. For some reason, the official history has combined the events of May 16 and 17 with what happened on May 18. Hickory was in response to the trouble 2/26 found itself in, and was also an attempt to surround and destroy the NVA forces in the area.

Reveille for 2/26 May 18 was at 0600H. The Marines were very tired and short of water. There had been so many losses that there were not enough men to cover the perimeter.[3] Early in the morning, the rest of the casualties from the day before were finally sent to the rear, resupply of ammunition and water also came in, and the new commanding officer, Masterpool, arrived.[4] Each American was again given only one canteen of water for the entire day.[5]

Three hours later Lt. Col. W. W. Vest's 3rd battalion, 4th Marines,[6] was taken by helicopter into the DMZ. The men landed near the Ben Hai River and were northwest of Con Thien.[7] Lt. Col. Vest's unit was to provide a blocking force in front of the advancing battalions of 2/26 and 2/9, while 3/9 would be protecting the operation's left flank. The mission of 3/4 was to prevent the escape or reinforcement of its foe.[8]

Elsewhere, Mitchell had gone to the platoon command post to pick up some c-rations and got caught in a mortar barrage:

"I was hoping that we didn't get a ground attack as I only had my 45-caliber pistol with me. I dove into a hole. The next thing I knew somebody jumped in on top of me. It was Dennis Moskal, our squad leader. We stayed down until the mortars lifted."[9]

This attack took place three and a half hours after reveille and was aimed at Foxtrot. Between fifteen and twenty 82mm mortar rounds killed two and wounded five U.S. troops from Foxtrot.[10]

Golf and Echo were once more ordered to lead the way. Foxtrot and the command group were to the rear and further back was Hotel. The lead companies saw twenty to twenty-five NVA soldiers running across the battalion front twenty minutes later. (Was this movement meant to draw the Marines forward?)[11] Mortar fire started to hail on the front line of the battalion right after it had formed up.[12] The Leathernecks fearlessly advanced, and the malicious exploding enemy mortar rounds followed them. The enemy had learned their lesson and were adjusting their mortars as 2/26 stormed forward. As the battalion got closer to its opponent's fortifications, it came under concentrated small arms fire. This fire thumped the front and right flank of the Marines. The mortar fire came in groups of about thirty rounds each. As soon as the counter-battery fire was brought onto the enemy's position, the mortar fire would cease. After running out of 60mm mortar shells, Oots found that firing LAW rockets (Light Assault Weapon; standard, shoulder-fired U.S. rocket)[13] in the direction from which the enemy fire was coming would also cause the NVA to stop shooting.[14] They were, however, merely relocating. When the enemy gunners took fire, they would pack up, move somewhere else and then resume their barrages.

A tank with Echo was struck by an RPG and set on fire, causing four casualties.[15] Cpl. John C. Chambers evacuated his wounded crew members and made sure they received treatment before he would allow the corpsmen to tend his injuries. He then jumped aboard the burning vehicle, with .50 caliber machine-gun rounds exploding on board, found the fire extinguisher and had an infantryman put out the fire. He and another Marine alternately fired the metallic monster's .30 caliber and .50 caliber machine guns and its 90mm cannon into the enemy position. Twice, heat and smoke forced him to exit the vehicle. However, he continued to return to the tracked machine and fire its armament. Before he and his crew were medevaced, he instructed an infantryman on the workings of the armored vehicle.[16] The tank continued in action[17] and Chambers was awarded the Silver Star.

CH-46A Sea Knight (*USMC*)

Dennis Moskal (*Author's Collection*)

M72 LAW (*U.S. Army*)

The riflemen were also having a hard time. Mitchell saw a mortar round flying through the air, about ten feet away, right before it burst. Four Americans near him were wounded.

"I jumped in a bomb crater" and "didn't have a scratch," said Mitchell.

His ears were ringing from the explosion.

Corporal Lyons was hit in the neck by a mortar fragment. The shrapnel in Lyons's neck was about the size of a half-dollar and a small portion of it was sticking out of the wound.

Short and stocky Platoon Commander Gerst yelled, "You're all right" to Lyons. Another Marine tried to pull the piece of metal out of "Bones's" neck. When he did blood started squirting out. Gerst saw what was happening and said, "Okay, go."[18]

Lyons went to the rear for treatment.

Tall and thin Pfc. Michael J. Cahalane, of Hamilton Ohio, had both of his legs blown off by mortar fire. He died six days later, while being evacuated by a C-130 transport plane.

So much for Mrs. Cahalane's nine months of pain and twenty years of hope.[19]

Another Leatherneck was ecstatic to have gotten "a million dollar wound." He was hit badly enough in the hand to be sent home, but was not crippled. He left for the rear with a giant grin on his face and was giggling with delight.[20] Bannister, who was in Mitchell's gun team, was hit in the posterior and was too embarrassed to tell the corpsmen. Eventually, Mitchell convinced Bannister to seek treatment. Later, Mitchell found the poncho on his pack had been torn by a bullet and a splinter of metal had been stopped by a packet of cocoa in his pocket.[21]

The corpsmen were busy, running around taking care of the mounting number of Marine casualties. One of them, Corpsman Robert A. Turner, of Portland, Maine, was taking care of the many wounded when he was hit in the shoulder and later died of shock.[22] The Platoon Diary said, 2/26 was "helpless under the mortar fire..."[23]

Mitchell, in the midst of the chaos, found himself in trouble:

> I didn't know how, but Jesse Fields and I got out ahead of everybody. We got to a hedgerow and got into a firefight with an NVA machine gun. We were shooting everything at

them and they were doing the same. We couldn't see them but knew where they were. We expended all of our ammo and all of the squad's ammo. I guess we won because the NVA's fire stopped, and we were still alive. I don't know if we killed them or they just pulled out. We pulled back to our lines.[24]

The U.S. troops called in air strikes and threw red smoke to mark the enemy targets. The jets hit the NVA positions fifty to seventy-five yards in front of the grunts. When Mitchell got back to the rest of Golf, he saw two Marines "about to fight over the contents of" a wounded grunt's pack.[25]

"I thought I'd die of thirst," said blond and boyish Chicoine. "We were so bad off that we stopped in a bamboo thicket, pulled out our bayonets, cut holes in the bamboo" and sucked out the moisture. He remembered it tasted like turpentine, but it kept them going.[26]

Due to the raging fire punishing the battalion from the right flank and right front, Masterpool decided to halt the battalion and wait until 2/9 could come up to protect that side.[27] This would also expand the frontage of the attack.[28] It was not until 1600H that Peeler's 2/9 was in position on 2/26's right.[29]

As the men of 2/26 waited for 2/9, dark clouds started moving in and the Leathernecks spread out their ponchos in the hope of catching some storm water. Some grunts used shell craters, others dug holes to put their ponchos in. A few of them rapidly built elaborate water traps. The initial shower was just enough to wash the dirt off the ponchos. The rain stopped and everyone groaned. Then, suddenly, a pouring cloudburst began. The men slaked their thirst and filled their canteens. It was manna from heaven.[30]

After 2/9 arrived, the Marines pounced with spirit onto the enemy defenders. The two battalions forged ahead using the road as a boundary, 2/26 to the left and 2/9 to the right. Peeler's 2/9 proceeded with Foxtrot and Hotel to the front and Echo and Golf to the rear, again a by-the-book frontal assault.[31]

They hit a wall of semi- and full-automatic fire and mortar rounds at 1630H. One of Mitchell's canteens had a four-inch rip made in it, but he was unhurt. An enemy soldier tried to hide from Pfc. George Valenti behind a banana tree. Valenti shot through the tree and killed him. Their opponents' fire was so torrid that the men of Golf took cover. Oots, the bullets flying around him, calmly walked up to the frontline, while talking on the radio. The grunts saw him, rose, and followed their captain.[32] The battalion continued to advance, with tanks ripping a path forward, and the Leathernecks overran the NVA position in the first hedgerow.

Gallantly the battalion then fell upon the second hedgerow.[33] There were six tanks with Golf Company and the North Vietnamese kept trying to demolish them. One of the armored vehicles attempted to go up and over a hedgerow, but slipped back down. As it did, either a 57mm recoilless or an RPG round fired from an enemy rampart behind the Marines flew over, missing the steel beast, and hitting the top of the second hedgerow.[34] "The round hit right by Mark Cauble," wrote Mitchell. "It looked like it blew him about three feet into the air and he was yelling."[35]

The force of the explosion lifted him up and tossed him like a rag doll, wrote Cauble. He thought his legs had been blown off. After lying on the ground for a moment, he checked himself for wounds and he seemed all right. When the explosion happened, Cauble had instinctively crossed his arms over his eyes. (More than thirty years later, he still picks small fragments of metal from his arms and face.) Pieces of hot metal had also set fire to areas of his clothing, but he patted out the flames with his hands. Cauble then looked around and saw that the Marines who had been near him were all covered in blood and moaning. Most of the shrapnel, strangely, had gone to the left and away from him.[36] Six men from 3rd Platoon were wounded by the explosion.[37] When Cauble, dazed and confused, staggered down to his fellow grunts, he found them discussing his demise.

One turned and said, "Well, here he is."

Cauble did not report his minor wounds.

The North Vietnamese had patiently waited for the Americans to pass by before they opened up. They had hoped to take out a tank before they were destroyed but had failed in the attempt. The Leathernecks located their position and brought up armor to finish them off.[38] After trekking about 100 yards from their starting point, 2/26 was finally stopped in its tracks by a solid sheet of mortar and small arms fire.[39]

Corpsman Robert A. Turner (*Brown Collection*)

Michael J. Cahalane on left (*Author's Collection*)

Bannister (*Author's Collection*)

Operation Hickory—collecting rain water (*Brown Collection*)

To the right, Peeler's battalion made contact with the enemy about an hour and a half later. Foxtrot and Hotel 2/9 came under sustained mortar and small arms fire. Hotel 2/9 suffered the severest losses with thirty-one wounded, including their company commander, Capt. Robert J. Thompson. The rest of the 2/9 lost one killed and eight disabled. They captured one hurt NVA soldier and two of 2/9's tanks were damaged by enemy fire and sent to the rear.[40] Screening the operation to the left, 3/9 advanced, but made no contact.

The battalion commanders of 2/26 and 2/9 decided to stop and form their men into defensive perimeters for the rest of the day.[41] Masterpool's 2/26 had suffered so many losses that 2/9 sent over its Foxtrot company as a reinforcement.[42]

That night the North Vietnamese put 2/26 to the test. Two firefights broke out, which resulted in three dead enemy soldiers.[43] Masterpool's 2/26 lost three killed and 104 wounded on May 18. The battalion had lost 261 of its 1,000 men. Twenty-six percent of the organization's complement was out of action. Only Hotel Company had not taken substantial casualties. Medevacs were now getting out without having to dodge enemy fire.[44] The Americans were about to drop from lack of sleep.[45] Determined to have plenty of water, many U.S. troops now carried as many as six full canteens.[46]

5

"We Were Like Sitting Ducks"

May 19

DURING THE NIGHT, the North Vietnamese had scattered and retreated in a northeasterly and northwesterly direction.[1] They covered their withdrawal with rear guard actions, and rocket and mortar fire. The enemy's execution of this retrograde movement was orderly and well coordinated. They would engage with the grunts and then retire before the Marines could come to grips with them. They were thus able to slip their major units back across the DMZ without too much trouble.[2]

The North Vietnamese knew that two USMC battalions had moved up to reinforce 2/26 and, no doubt, were aware that another U.S. unit had landed behind them. This information had likely prompted them to break off the action and move out of the box the Leathernecks were trying to put them in. Stiff fighting, though, was still ahead for the Americans.

Fosmo was heating a cup of coffee on the morning of May 19 when he received a visitor.

> A Marine who I thought was a staff NCO or something stopped and told me he liked my hooch and we visited awhile. He had on skivvies with hearts all over them, flak vest and helmet. Later I found out he was Lt. Col. Masterpool; he was an all-right guy.[3]

The Marines moved out at 0700H.[4] Golf and Echo of 2/26 proceeded on the left and Hotel and Foxtrot of 2/9 covered the right. The two battalions were again using the road as a boundary. As the U.S. troops pushed ahead, they met little resistance. While they continued to be mortared, it was not as bad as before.[5] Golf 2/26 took the brunt of the bombardment. Ten NVA 60mm mortar rounds heartlessly lashed Golf an hour later, striking sixteen

Leathernecks. Another volley, this time fifteen to twenty 82mm rounds, wounded eighteen, including a female correspondent.[6]

Attractive twenty-two-year-old Catherine Leroy of France was the injured photographer. She had come in on one of the first Medevacs around May 16-17. When she arrived, she wore black fatigues and had her own pack and e-tool.[7]

"My size six foot was swimming in my size seven jungle boots, the smallest they had. There was nothing sexy about me," she said.

The grunts would not have agreed. To them she was a beautiful and mysterious apparition. Her brown hair was in pigtails. She stood five feet tall and weighed eighty-five pounds.[8] Cauble saw the diminutive and energetic journalist bouncing around taking pictures all over the battlefield.[9] Leroy carried three cameras around her neck: a Nikon, a Nikormat, and a Leica. Oots assigned Brown to her.

Brown remembered how exposed they were during the mortar bombardment, "We were like sitting ducks."

The same mortar round hit both of them.

Leroy said, "I was hit by the first mortar. In my head it was a big sound...like a gong. I knew I was hit but was still on my feet. I felt nothing but noticed my right pigtail was all blood. My three cameras were also bloody...They had been hit and probably saved my life.

"It seemed like five minutes before anyone saw me. I was really groggy and in bad shape. I couldn't breath and was bleeding all over. I thought I was going to die.

"They started to cut off my fatigues and take off my bra. I was never so embarrassed in my life and kept saying...no...no...no!

"Someone said, 'This is no time for modesty,' and then it was all right."[10]

"I had one piece of shrapnel hit me in my right arm. She had thirty-five holes in her," Brown recalled.

Leroy also had her jaw broken. Brown believed the cameras saved her life because "they absorbed a lot of shrapnel." Brown and Leroy were put on tanks and taken to Con Thien, where helicopters took them "to the battalion aid station in Dong Ha. From there we both went to the hospital ship *U.S.S. Sanctuary.*"[11]

Operation Hickory—Cathy Leroy, Martinez, Oots (*Brown Collection*)

Staff Sgt. Russ Havourd of S*tars And Stripes* reported, "Cathy...underwent a three-hour operation to remove the shrapnel. She still has multiple scars on her legs, neck, arms, chest, back, and face..."[12]

Six weeks later Ms. Leroy was back in the bush. Her dedication impressed Brown.

"When I think of her," said Brown, "I wonder what makes a person do what she did. Reporters and photographers, I guess, are strange people in a sense. I first thought that she might be a little crazy for wanting to be in Vietnam, and I even thought that she had to be stupid. But that's not it at all. She is far from either one, but there is something that drives these people."[13]

Elsewhere, another Marine had a lucky escape.

At one point in the bombardment, Cauble was seized by the insane impulse to look up at the falling mortar rounds. He got to see a great show, with explosions striking all around him. Fortunately, he wasn't hit and he never repeated this foolish act.[14]

Martinez was again helping evacuate casualties when he was lacerated in the leg by darting metal. He refused to be medevaced and continued to assist hurt Marines. For his courageous efforts over the past four days Martinez was awarded the Silver Star.[15] As the wounded were being moved the grunts found thirty-two newly buried NVA bodies. They also saw two dead North Vietnamese next to a 57mm recoilless rifle. Two hours later, an Ontos rolled over a mine, and a massive eruption of fire and smoke engulfed the vehicle, killing one Marine and wounding seven more. As the Americans advanced, they found numerous strongly built NVA bunkers. An enemy straggler was killed in one of the abandoned positions.[16]

Early in the afternoon 2/26 stopped, formed a perimeter and fortified for the night.[17] Foxtrot and Hotel moved in front of Golf and Echo. The battalion was in a box formation.[18] Golf was hit by thirty rounds of 105mm enemy artillery fire at 1850H.[19] The U.S. troops put a forward observer into a tree to pinpoint the enemy artillery positions. From where the Leathernecks were, they could see across the Ben Hai River and into the DMZ.[20] Air and artillery strikes took out two North Vietnamese guns and damaged three more, killing twenty-five North Vietnamese.[21] The grunts saw their foe moving trucks down to pull their guns out when American fire started to savage them.

About twenty minutes later Hotel Company 2/9 had their right flank torn up by NVA mortar rounds and automatic fire. The Marines returned fire and requested tanks. When the armor arrived they fired canister point blank into the enemy. The NVA immediately stopped firing and a U.S. squad was sent forward to scout the emplacement. The enemy had been playing possum, opened up again and trapped the grunts in the dried-up rice paddy. The two tracked vehicles moved up to rescue the Americans.[22] The North Vietnamese had what they wanted, USMC vehicles in range of their anti-tank weapons.

While the armor rattled and clanked toward their fate, Cpl. Richard K. Gillingham of H Company 2/9 audaciously ran twenty yards forward to rescue one of his men who had been wounded. Gillingham was hit three different times trying to help his comrade. Despite his injuries, he brought the injured Marine back to safety. Gillingham died from his wounds while attempting to rejoin his squad. Gillingham, for his courage, was posthumously awarded the Silver Star.[23]

Meanwhile, to the right, Sgt. William Baxter Gilley, squad leader of 2nd Platoon, Foxtrot 2/9, led his squad in a turning maneuver against the NVA. Four times he intrepidly led his squad forward and four times they were driven back by scalding enemy fire. After the last attempt, he found out that a member of his squad had been severely wounded and left behind. Gilley located the disabled Marine and charged into the open to rescue him. The North Vietnamese spotted him and opened fire. Gilley was badly gashed in the leg, but continued forward to the hurt Marine. Reaching his comrade, he lifted the wounded man onto his shoulders and ran back to his squad. For his remarkable efforts Gilley was awarded the Silver Star.[24]

The tanks sent to help the Marines were destroyed by enemy fire and both U.S. companies fell back carrying their casualties. Supporting fire was requested to pulverize the enemy entrenchments. Seven Marines were killed and twelve were wounded in this firefight.[25] Off to the left, 3/9 made no contact. Nor did 3/4, which was acting as a blocking force to the north.

As night fell, Golf 2/26 combined its three platoons into one. The company only had seventy-six men left.[26] The men of 2/26 lost one killed and forty-five wounded on May 19. The four-day total for the battalion was 307 killed and wounded. About thirty percent of the unit's strength had been lost. They counted sixty-two lifeless North Vietnamese.[27] With most of the People's Army out of the area, the Leathernecks could relax a bit. Thinking back, Cauble realized he hadn't relieved himself even once over the past four days. The grunts were mentally and physically exhausted, but that night they would get some sleep.[28]

6

"Calmly Accepting the Consequences of Their Action"

May 20 and May 21

THE STRUGGLE CONTINUED on May 20. After air and artillery strikes, the Marines thrust against the NVA ramparts to their front. The two battalions were still using the road as a boundary; 2/26 was to the left and 2/9 was to the right. Smarting from the "bloody nose" it had received on May 19, 2/9 charged forward and found that the enemy had abandoned their battlements. Likewise, 2/26 made no contact.[1] The Americans advanced about 500 meters and constructed earthworks. They stopped and remained where they were for the balance of that day. The two battalions also stayed in place the next day.[2] Patrols were sent out desperately looking for water. One of these patrols located a mountain stream and the Americans were able to fill their canteens.[3]

Meanwhile, the 3rd Marine Division Reserve, 2nd Battalion, 3rd Regiment, commanded by Lt. Col Earl R. DeLong, joined Operation Hickory. The Marines were brought in by helicopter on May 20, northwest of Gio Ling, to block escape routes of enemy units engaged with Army of the Republic of Vietnam forces. They failed to locate and engage their foe.[4]

The same day 3/9 ran into serious action. Some of the North Vietnamese retreated to the northwest and 3/9, screening the western flank of the operation, moved north. They inevitably ran into each other. Wilson of 3/9 had K Company leading the way when they made contact with a People's Army rearguard of company strength at least. The enemy was fortified and put out a deadly fire on the advancing Marines.[5] Cpl. Walter J. Washut's platoon became isolated from the rest of the battalion and took many casualties. While only a squad leader, he took command and deployed the platoon. Washut was able to direct an effective fire on the NVA and extract his men from their dangerous position.

After reaching his own lines he continued to head the platoon with dash and to rally his men. He spotted an enemy mortar position and single-handedly destroyed it with a LAW rocket. An injured Marine in front of the enemy position caught his attention and he ran, under fire, to his rescue. When he reached the disabled man he found other injured Americans nearby. He directed their removal and began to bandage the suffering grunt he had first gone to help. While binding the wounds of his comrade, Washut was ripped apart by enemy fire and killed. For his leadership and loyalty he was posthumously awarded the Silver Star.[6] After this, Wilson had his L Company swing around and strike the enemy flank. Darkness had fallen and they were unable to link up with K Company.[7]

That night the machine gun team of Lance Cpl. David G. Bendorf and Pfc. David E. Hartsoe volunteered to lead Company L to Company K. As they moved forward in the dark, they came under fierce NVA fire. They set up their gun at the very front of the company and opened fire. The men of Lima took many casualties in the following firefight and decided to retreat. Bendorf and Hartsoe tenaciously stayed, to cover the recovery of wounded and their comrades' withdrawal, "calmly accepting the consequences of their action."[8] As the grunts retired, they heard short, controlled bursts of fire from the machine gun team. The enemy concentrated their forces and launched an overwhelming attack on the two men. Bendorf and Hartsoe died at their post. For their sacrifice they were both posthumously awarded the Navy Cross.[9]

The two U.S. companies lost twenty-six killed and fifty-nine wounded. During the night air strikes and artillery fire pummeled the enemy dugouts. The next day M Company was sent forward to reinforce K and L. Together the three companies swept through the enemy position, but the Reds had gone. The USMC found the remains of thirty-six enemy soldiers.[10]

At the same time, 2/26, after a much-needed rest, was ready to move.

7

"Into the DMZ"

May 22 – 24

AFTER 3/4 AND 2/26 had been given a brief respite, they started traveling southwest through the DMZ. The two battalions were advancing "toward the mountains west of Con Thien."[1] Moving through the bush was difficult at best. The worst obstacles were at crossings. Walking over swaying bamboo bridges and balancing on teetering logs would always increase the heart rate.[2] Meanwhile, 3/9 again marched to the northwest. The other units committed to Operation Hickory, swept "the southern half of the DMZ and Leatherneck Square."[3] On May 22, 2/9 left 2/26 and resumed its original mission as regimental reserve.[4]

Golf Company dispatched patrols into the DMZ the same day.[5] The battalion then proceeded down the west side of Con Thien.[6] The grunts walked parallel to a road using the tanks to clear a way for them. The dirt path was avoided because it was assumed to be mined. The stifling temperature and humidity caused a number of heat prostration and heat stroke cases.[7]

The extremely tired Marines stayed in fieldworks for the next few days in what had been an agricultural development center. On May 24, Echo and Hotel moved north into the DMZ. There was a stream on the southern boundary of the DMZ that their tanks were unable to cross. The armor, as a result, was sent back to Con Thien. Foxtrot and Golf formed the rear part of the battalion's perimeter south of the brook.[8] Throughout the sweep the U.S. troops met little resistance, but found numerous enemy redoubts and equipment. The grunts also killed a few stray NVA soldiers and found several opponents' bodies.[9]

2/26 had an excellent forward observer, Sgt. Moon, and he was known for his ability to put artillery fire right on target. The Americans were told he was already supposed to have gone home.

Moon decided, because of the continuing enemy threat, to stay with 2/26 until the operation was over. Not many would have made that choice.[10]

The Leathernecks were reminded from time to time that, they were in a jungle after all. As the Marines moved through some heavy brush, California native Chicoine saw a tiger about fifty meters from him. He wasn't worried because he was carrying an M-60 machine gun and the tiger moved off, back into the foliage, without incident.[11] Fortunately, these encounters were rare. Golf Company had several unusual occurrences with animals and insects.

Earlier that year a tiger had broken into a mess hall and had run off with a side of beef that had been left out to defrost. The tiger, with the beef between its jaws, easily jumped an eight-foot fence to get away. Some time later another tiger stealthily moved inside a night ambush and started to drag off a sleeping Marine by his foot. He awoke and opened fire. The tiger dropped his prey and ran.[12] Tigers were not the only animals to fear.

Two wild enraged water buffalos attacked 3rd Platoon and hurt two men before a torrent of bullets took the beasts down.[13]

When Golf was stationed in a bunker complex it had to live with rats. A few of these creatures were the size of small cats. At night the men could feel the vermin scurrying across their bodies. Some of the rodents were brazen enough to steal food while the Marines were eating. The grunts found a cat and used it to clean out the complex one position at a time. The last bunker had a huge and fearless "king" rat. The men had become fond of this rodent and respected its courage. The Marines even bet on who would win the showdown. The fight was loud and furious. The rodent won and the cat fled – never to be seen again.

Mosquitoes and leeches were an ongoing nuisance. Mosquitoes could suck the Leathernecks' blood right through their clothes and their hands became lumpy from the bites. The men were given mosquito repellent, but sometimes they ran out and they could not put it on their lips because it would burn them. On one occasion, a grunt's lips were so swollen from bites that he was unable to speak clearly.

There were both land and water leeches and they varied in size and color from less than an inch and dark brown to giant red and

green foot-long monsters. During one operation a Marine woke up
to find the tail of a leech sticking out the end of his penis. When he
tried to grab the tail, the leech shot up into his urinary canal and he
had to be hospitalized. During a firefight Cauble had to take cover
in a rice paddy. He lay down and the water was up to his chin.
Cauble was too busy dodging enemy fire to notice that a foot-long
leech had slithered up his neck and wrapped itself around his head.
A short time after the skirmish, a corpsman noticed blood
streaming down the Marine's neck. The corpsman took off the
Leatherneck's helmet and started to examine the "wound."

The corpsman asked, "How did you get hit there?"

Then Cauble looked down and saw the huge leech in his helmet
and the mystery was solved.

Danger also lurked from above and below. While cutting their
way through the jungle a beehive fell on a platoon and the Marines
had to fight both the jungle and the bees. While digging
entrenchments in the mountains, the Leathernecks unearthed a
yard-long yellow and red centipede; they were so startled that they
shot the bug up with their M-16s.[14] These distractions were
another facet of life in the bush. The grunts had enough trouble
with the enemy without having to worry about the local wildlife.

Near dark on May 24, Cauble, who later became a college
instructor and was ironically enough referred to as "professor,"
was sent with a patrol down to the creek that bordered the DMZ to
replenish his platoon's canteens. The Marines crossed over to the
north bank of the stream so they could later say they had been in
the DMZ.[15]

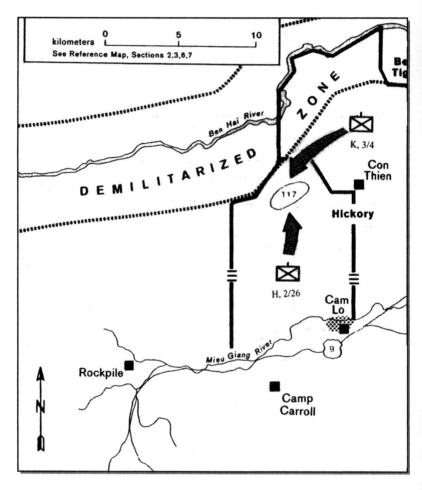

Hill 117, May 25-27 (*USMC*)

8

Hill 117

May 25 – 27

HOTEL COMPANY had marched all day May 24, wrote Tom Lehner, through "thickly forested hills" before stopping for the night. They were inside the DMZ and knew it.[1] The other companies in 2/26 had made heavy contact and the men of Hotel were "nervous" because they knew their turn had come, recalled Hancock.[2] Even though they had not been heavily engaged, attrition from enemy artillery, mortar and rocket fire had reduced Hotel to about 150 men.[3] At 0200H the next day, mortar rounds started dropping on Hotel's perimeter. The North Vietnamese were so close that the muzzle flash from their mortar could be seen and the light silhouetted the gun team. Spotting the mortar's position, Sergeant Ralph Gomez opened fire. By using his tracer rounds to adjust his fire, he was able to silence the foe's position.

Capt. John J. Rozman's Hotel Company was about to engage several companies of well-dug-in North Vietnamese.[4] Hotel faced Hill 117, with 3rd Platoon on the left and 2nd Platoon on the right. Rozman kept his 1st Platoon in reserve.

Lehner, who was the radio operator for Lieutenant James McGill of 2nd Platoon, remembered how the fight started:

> As first light broke May 25, 1967, a squad from the 3rd Platoon of Hotel, which had been sent out on an outpost, began taking fire as they exited the wood line of Hill 117. Another squad was sent to their assistance. Their location was on the far left of the hill. 2nd Platoon occupied the far right of the perimeter. Lt. James McGill got the call to lead a column of his troops into the wood line to his front and then have his troops make a left face and do an enveloping maneuver towards the pinned-down squads of 3rd Platoon. McGill quickly spat out the order to the troops and, with .45

drawn, took the point as he led the column towards the wood line at double time. One step into the wood line, firing broke out and McGill was shot through the mouth with a wound that exited the back of his head. While the corpsman, Mel Overmyer, moved up to work on McGill, the remainder of the platoon, which was now under the command of Sgt. Llewellan, fanned out on both sides of McGill. They began to probe the wood line and either gunfire or grenades met every probe. Several Marines were wounded severely. Some were blown out of the wood line several times by the impact of the grenades but continued to probe the line.[5]

Machine gunner Chicoine said, "I was really tearing up the countryside." The Marines were flat on the ground "and crawling forward once in a while." Even though the grunts were not moving around much, he remembered, "I was more tired than I think I had ever been in my life. It seemed like every bit of energy was drained out of me."[6]

Hancock's squad was flank protection and was having a hard time hacking through the jungle when the battle started:

We got what seemed to me to be about half way up the hill when the firing started to our left (which gave us the split second we needed to get down), then all hell broke loose. It seemed like the whole hillside opened up on us. The NVA were only about ten or fifteen yards away from us in concealed fighting holes and trenches. They started lobbing grenades down at us. Several of the men were wounded. We started putting out as much fire as we could to try to suppress their fire. It wasn't working like it had on the VC. I remember the AK-47 rounds were coming in such volume it seemed like I could feel the heat from the rounds going close overhead. Small branches and twigs from the bush I was under were falling down my neck and back from the rounds knocking them off. We started throwing grenades. I saw several NVA moving from one position to another. The others must have seen them also, and we fired in their direction. They dropped (I'm not positive if they were hit or dove for cover, but we put a lot of fire on them and in my mind they were hit). I'm not sure how long it lasted, but every time the fire started slacking from their side, we tried moving up, and it would pick up again. It seemed like an eternity.[7]

The Americans tried to advance, but they were taking cruel losses.

Lehner wrote, "Two Marines, Lance Cpl. Ray Sieger and Pfc. Peter Coons were shot dead while trying to pinpoint the enemy fire. Corpsman Overmyer continued to work on McGill despite being in the line of fire. Eventually, Overmyer received a head wound and staggered from the wood line with the mortally wounded McGill. The corpsman was later recommended for the Silver Star."[8]

Hotel Company was ordered to retreat. The U.S. troops carried their dead and injured off the hill.[9]

Artillery and air strikes covered the hill with explosions and firey napalm. Capt. John H. Flathman's Company K, 3/4 was sent to reinforce Hotel.[10] The other companies of 2/26 were obviously considered too weak by higher command to help their sister unit. Company H, 2/26 moved around to the north of Hill 117 and linked up with Kilo 3/4 at 1345H. The two companies then assaulted the Hill together.[11]

"Everyone was really on edge now," said Hancock.[12]

It no longer became a question of "would he get wounded?" wrote Chicoine, but "when and how bad?"[13] The Marines encountered heavy fire at 1500H.[14]

Lehner remembered that this new attempt fared no better then the last: "This time the Marines were able to enter the wood line, but it was not long before they again ran into the NVA and their fortified bunkers.... Men were killed and wounded by an enemy they could not see. Once contact was made, every inch of forward movement seemed to produce a casualty.... Again the order to withdraw came and again they carried their fallen comrades from the scene."

A machine gunner from Hotel had "most of his fingers shot off," said then nineteen-year-old Chicoine.

"He was wandering around with a smile on his face saying, 'I'm going home, I'm going home' over and over."

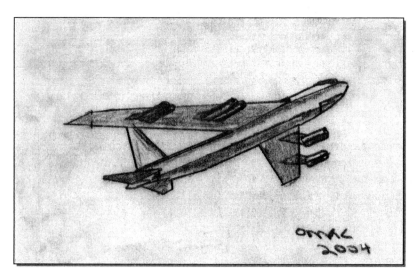

B-52 bomber

Masterpool ordered them to fall back. Before launching another assault, Masterpool wanted to flatten the hill, an idea he said, "which was very popular among the troops."[15] That night B-52 heavy bombers leveled the hill with 2000-pound bombs.[16] The thundering explosions lit up the sky, turning night into day.[17]

The next morning, Hancock recalled, "The hill had almost been blown bare of plant life."[18]

Hotel had lost almost a third of its men, with five killed and over forty disabled.[19] Kilo was even worse off, with nine killed and about fifty hurt.[20]

Masterpool decided to fly over the hill, with executive officer Landers, to assess the damage. On the way he had his UH-1E helicopter land and pickup Rozman and Flathman.[21] After they lifted off, they started to receive heavy machine gun fire. The pilot was maneuvering the helicopter to avoid this threat, when anti-aircraft artillery rounds pelted them. The pilot was gashed in the neck and the co-pilot was injured in the right side. Masterpool was also hit. The helicopter fell like a stone. Masterpool said that the pilot, though wounded, showed "no panic, no confusion" and brought the copter safely down "right into Indian country." They had gone down so fast that they had been unable to issue a distress call.

Covered in blood, Masterpool got out of the helicopter and realized, "boy we are in real trouble out here."

Luckily, they had been spotted going down and were quickly lifted out.[22] Both Masterpool and Flathman were badly hit and had to be evacuated. As a result, the planned attack had to be called off, while "command adjustments" took place. Landers again took command of 2/26.[23] Hotel 2/26 and Kilo 3/4 were transferred from 2/26 to the operational control of Vest's 3/4 on May 26.[24] All during May 26, artillery and air pounded Hill 117.

A further realignment took place the next day when Echo and Foxtrot 2/26 were also given to Vest. This left Landers with only Golf Company. Echo and Foxtrot moved up the hill on May 27.[25] Echo Company took the lead with Foxtrot to the rear. The two companies were told to use as much supporting fire as they wanted. Fulford called in fire 100 meters ahead of his front line. He would not move his company forward until the area ahead had been smashed by shells. Over 1000 artillery and mortar rounds were expended in the advance. Surprisingly, the enemy was gone. There was evidence that the North Vietnamese had run out in a hurry. While the enemy left a lot of captured American gear behind, they left none of their own equipment. The two companies spent the next few days on the hill scouting the area.[26] Echo and Foxtrot discovered more than forty NVA bunkers.[27] The Marines also found forty-one dead enemy troops on the hill.[28]

As Golf 2/26 moved around the hill, Cauble remembered walking past a crater caused by a 2000-pound bomb. The hole was large enough to fit a tank inside. It was so deep, he thought, if you lost your balance and fell into the pit, you would break your leg. The terrain looked like a gigantic plow had gone through the area and turned the soil. Trees were completely uprooted and all the vegetation had been swept away. Everywhere he looked there was only dirt and craters. What had been a lush jungle was now a moonscape.[29]

Hotel's time had come and now all four of 2/26's rifle companies had been through the "meat grinder." The battalion had lost 352 men, or around thirty-five percent of its strength. The men were spent.

9

"Men Are About Pooped"

May 27 – June 4

GOLF COMPANY MOVED about 2,000 meters May 27 and reorganized itself into two small platoons. 1st Platoon diary stated, "men are about pooped."[1] The new commander of 2/26, Lt. Col. Duncan D. Chaplin III, arrived that morning.[2] The thirty-nine-year-old New Hampshire native was a caring and humorous individual, who immediately made a favorable impression on his men. Very soon the Marines were writing "Chaplin's Nomads" on their helmets. The rumor at the time was that the name signified that the unit had no home base.[3]

"The battalion," Chaplin wrote, "was pretty black and blue but held together by a leadership core of combat survivors."[4]

Patrols continued the next day and more than ninety enemy bunkers were located and destroyed. The battalion command post was hit by ten 140mm rockets, and Marine mortars and artillery returned fire.[5]

Fulford remembered that the rockets were extremely inaccurate, "I don't believe a single person in the battalion was hit." [6]

At midnight May 28, Operation Hickory came to a conclusion. The U.S. had 142 killed and 896 wounded in the operation. ARVN losses totaled twenty-two dead and 122 injured. The NVA lost 789 dead and thirty-seven captured. About 11,000 civilians were relocated from the area. The operation represented a major escalation in the war. From now on American and South Vietnamese forces would move into the DMZ to pursue enemy forces and break up concentrations of NVA. The U.S. Marines now resumed Prairie IV.[7] From May 29 to 31, 2/26 patrolled around the agricultural center and Hill 117.[8] Golf Company's 1st Platoon, May 31, moved onto Hill 162.[9] It was to be, as Mitchell wrote, "another bad day."

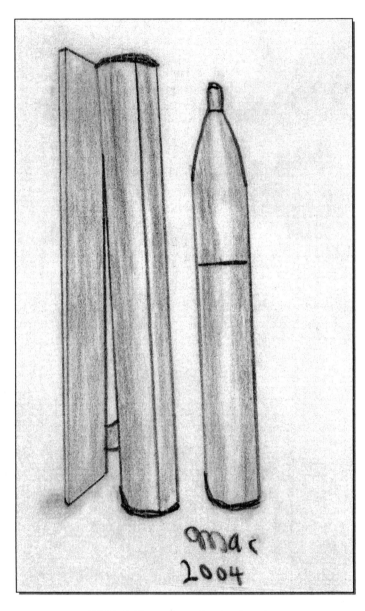

NVA 140mm launcher and rocket

The point was taken by squad leader Lance Cpl. Dennis C. Johnson of Twain Harte, California. His tour was almost over. He was about to go home.

Normally, Johnson was deliberate when going through hostile territory, but for some reason there was a rush to get to the top. Near the summit, at 1440H, there was an explosion. Johnson tripped a mine killing him and hitting four other men. About an hour later, when the U.S. troops reached the crest, another explosive was set off, disabling two more Americans. The entire hill had been booby-trapped. A tank was sent up the hill to crush the remaining mines.[10] The men wondered if the horror would ever end.

Prairie IV ended on May 31[11] and Operation Cimarron commenced one day later.[12] That afternoon a helicopter brought two generals in to visit the troops, and they praised the men for their efforts. Most of the Leathernecks were in a state of disbelief; they were not used to being around generals. However, some of the men felt comfortable and even had pictures taken standing with the top brass.[13] The Marines ran patrols on June 2, and the next day they moved off the hill and swept south with the rest of the battalion back down to Highway Nine and the Cam Lo area.[14] 2/26 moved two companies abreast, with 1,000 meters between them. Protecting the left was 3/9, and screening the right was 3/4.

Fulford remembered that as the U.S. troops advanced, the companies would leapfrog each other. The lead companies would advance 2000-3000 meters and then stop to allow the rear companies to move through them and assume the point and so on. As the Americans advanced, they used artillery to clear the way. This was the reason, Fulford believed, that they made little contact on their southward sweep.[15] Actually, the enemy had already withdrawn from the area.

Throughout this move south, 2/26 received large amounts of resupply. The Marines picked what they wanted out of the cases of c-rations and threw the rest away. Gallon cans of fruit in heavy syrup were distributed and the joyful grunts quickly devoured their favorite delicacy.[16]

The battalion reached the Cam Lo area on June 4 and spent the night.[17]

2/26 had thirty-seven dead and 324 wounded, more than thirty-six percent of the battalion's strength. The grunts had killed 207 of the enemy.[18]

The number of injured Leathernecks cited above does not represent all those who were hit. Almost all the Americans had received multiple wounds, but had stopped reporting them after the first day of combat, and those who were not sent to the rear for treatment are not included in this total. For example, counting walking wounded, Golf had 157 men injured and only forty who had not been harmed.[19] Cauble recalled and Chaplin confirmed, that only 206 men in the battalion had been untouched by fire, which means, out of a total force of about 1000, casualties were, in fact, around 800.[20] Mitchell was one of the exceptions; he escaped from the ordeal unscathed.

The men of 2/26 were drained, emotionally, physically and mentally. They needed the break they were about to get.

10

"He Was a Good Captain"

June 5 – June 9

THE SURVIVORS from 2/26 boarded trucks the morning of June 5 for transport to Phu Bai. They had taken part in three operations, Prairie IV, Hickory and Cimarron, but would always refer to the experience as Hickory. The battalion would be taking over the defense of Phu Bai from 3rd Battalion, 26th Marines, which was heading north.[1]

The grunts were very happy to leave. Cauble remembered an almost festive atmosphere on his truck. One Leatherneck took the elastic string out of his field jacket and tied it to an empty c-ration can. He would throw it at Vietnamese children as he drove by them and they would dive for the can. He would then pull it back, with the attached string, and it would snap back into the truck before they could grab the can. Each time he did this the entire truckload of Americans would explode with hysterical laughter.[2] When the U.S. troops arrived at Phu Bai, they were given showers, new clothes, a hot meal and beer.[3]

"We were treated like heroes," wrote Wickersham.[4]

The men rested, got back mail and more beer over the next two days.

Oots was transferred to S-4 June 8. Both Oots and the sixty-six men left in Golf Company were near tears over his leaving.

The platoon diary stated, "He was a good Captain."[5]

This affection, devotion and respect were earned. One can only remark that the leadership displayed by Marine officers was exceptional and that they fought like lions. Let us not forget the rank and file who had also distinguished themselves and upheld the finest traditions of the Corps.

The next day brought "more gear and beer" and the news that the battalion was going to receive a citation.[6] Vice President

Hubert Humphrey was to present the 3rd Marine Division with the Presidential Unit Citation on November 1, 1967. Operation Hickory was part of that award.[7]

The holiday came to an end when 2/26 left for Operation Sparrow Hawk on June 10.[8]

Mitchell, who had the misfortune to be on both Operation Hickory and at the famous 1968 siege of Khe Sanh,[9] compared the two battles: "I don't think Khe Sanh was as bad as Operation Hickory."[10]

It was a time no one who was there will ever forget.

Oots saying good-bye to the troops (*Brown Collection*)

They were a scary group, these Marines. The men were grimy and covered in blood. As the rags they wore billowed around their emaciated bodies, Golf Company staggered off the trucks and formed up. Everyone was amazed at how few they were, not even a platoon left out of a company. The grunts stacked their equipment where they stood. Then they marched over to tents where they stripped off what was left of their uniforms, and washed off the dirt and gore. Given new utilities and a hot meal, the Leathernecks lay on their racks, wrote letters and drifted off to sleep. They were alive.[11]

Part III

Epilogue

End Game

DURING THE LAST SIX MONTHS of 1967, the North Vietnamese tried twice more to take Con Thien. Each time they were driven back with heavy losses.[1] The enemy's biggest blow was yet to come.

The turning point in Vietnam was the Tet Offensive. On January 31, 1968, the Reds broke a holiday truce and launched attacks throughout South Vietnam.[2] The city of Hue fell to the NVA and Viet Cong, and they temporarily occupied the grounds of the U.S. Embassy in Saigon. Militarily, Westmoreland said the offensive was a major debacle for the enemy.[3] However, the impact on the U.S. public was devastating. The American press and people saw Tet as an American disaster. They thought the U.S. was close to winning the war, and the massive Red attack, even through it was repelled, was seen as a defeat. *The New York Times* and *Wall Street Journal* newspapers, and *Time*, *Newsweek*, *Atlantic* and *Harper's* magazines, called for an American withdrawal.[4] Newscaster Walter Cronkite told the public that the war couldn't be won.[5]

President Johnson remarked, "If I've lost Walter then I've lost Mr. Average Citizen."[6]

Polls showed Johnson's popularity had declined to less than forty percent[7] and Senator Eugene McCarthy of Minnesota announced his decision to oppose the President in the Democratic primaries.[8] The first primary took place in New Hampshire and McCarthy received forty-two percent of the vote to LBJ's forty-nine percent.[9] As a result, Robert Kennedy announced that he would seek the Democratic nomination for president.[10] Johnson went on television two months later, and told the American people he was stopping the bombing of North Vietnam and that the U.S. would attempt a new peace initiative. LBJ also announced that he would not run for a second term. The North Vietnamese agreed to

negotiate and peace talks began in Paris May 10, 1968.[11] The quest
for military victory had ended and the new dilemma for the
American government was how to get out of Vietnam with a
minimum of damage to U.S. prestige.

Richard M. Nixon was elected President of the United States in
November 1968.[12] While campaigning, he claimed to have a secret
plan that would bring "peace with honor."[13] When he became
president, Nixon executed his plans on three fronts. American
negotiators at the Paris Peace Talks insisted on the return of
American prisoners of war, communist withdrawal from South
Vietnam and the preservation of the South Vietnamese
government. The North Vietnamese and Viet Cong were adamant
about staying in South Vietnam and on the reunification of
Vietnam under a communist government. Nixon also moved to
quell domestic unrest over the war. He reduced the number of
American troops and began "Vietnamization." Vietnamization was
a beefing up of South Vietnam's military, so they would be able to
defend themselves. Nixon started in office with 540,000 American
troops in Vietnam.[14] By 1972, the number of U.S. military forces
had dropped to 70,000.[15] The president also persuaded Congress to
end the draft and instituted an all-volunteer force. This undercut
the anti-war movement. Beginning in March 1972, the North
Vietnamese tested Vietnamization by launching a massive
invasion of the South.[16] With the assistance of U.S. air power, the
South Vietnamese were able to defeat the Reds by mid-July.
Nixon was on the way to creating a self-sufficient South Vietnam,
protected by U.S. planes and a small U.S. ground force. Time was
now on Nixon's side. Finally, while reducing the number of
American troops, Nixon intensified and expanded the air war to
cover the United States' withdrawal, and to convince the North
Vietnamese to come to terms. During the summer of 1972,
Secretary of State Henry Kissinger started meeting secretly with
Le Duc Tho, the chief North Vietnamese negotiator. On October
26, 1972, a week before the presidential election, Kissinger
announced that "peace was at hand." The North Vietnamese had
agreed to our demands eighteen days earlier.[17] The terms were an
immediate cease-fire, the South Vietnamese government would
continue in power, the U.S. would withdraw its forces, American
prisoners of war would be returned, and there would be no further

communist infiltration. The North Vietnamese accepted twelve changes to the agreement on November 23. They abruptly withdrew their agreement to these changes December 12.

Winston Lord, one of the U.S. negotiators, said, "Specifically in December it was clear that the North Vietnamese were sliding away from an agreement."[18]

The peace talks were broken off on December 13. Nixon ordered B-52 strikes on Hanoi to get the communists back to the peace table. December 18-29, American planes bombed Hanoi. Twenty-six planes were lost and 1600 civilians killed. The North Vietnamese returned to the peace talks and agreed to accept the November 23 changes.

Lord, reflecting on the bombing said, "It did achieve the breakthrough, and there's no other explanation for Hanoi changing its attitude."[19]

The agreement to end the war was signed January 23, 1973, in Paris. The last U.S. combat troop left South Vietnam two months later, and several hundred American POWs were returned. The United States promised to continue to aid and give air support to South Vietnam.

Nixon's Watergate scandal would soon have disastrous consequences for South Vietnam. As Nixon's political troubles increased, the Democrat-controlled Congress asserted itself. Congress stopped all U.S. bombing in support of South Vietnam during June 1973. Furthermore, Congress cut aid to South Vietnam from $20 billion to $1 billion the next year. Nixon resigned because of Watergate, August 1974, and Vice President Gerald Ford became President. The Congressional elections that year saw a veto-proof liberal Democratic majority swept into office. During 1975 Congress cut off all aid to South Vietnam. Outnumbered, out-gunned and with no help from the U.S., South Vietnam was overwhelmed by the Reds. The last Americans were evacuated from Saigon April 28, 1975. The North Vietnamese completed their conquest two days later.

From 1965 to 1973, the U.S. lost 58,000 dead and the North Vietnamese suffered around one million killed.[20]

Nixon, Kissinger and Westmoreland maintained that, but for Watergate, South Vietnam would be a free republic today.[21] One must ask, is it reasonable to assume, even without Watergate, that

America would have maintained its resolve and continued to support South Vietnam indefinitely?

Westmoreland also believed that graduated response had been a mistake, as was the failure to move into "Laos and Cambodia and north of the DMZ, along with intensified bombing and the mining of Haiphong Harbor" after the defeat of the Tet Offensive.[22]

Massive air power, as Nixon's "Christmas bombing" showed, could have an influence and Col. Harry G. Summers, Jr., in his book *On Strategy: The Vietnam War in Context*, supports Westmoreland's offensive concept.[23] Johnson, Westmoreland said, was unduly afraid of Soviet and Chinese intervention and would not agree to his plan.[24] It is impossible to know how the Soviets and communist Mainland Chinese might have reacted or what may have developed from this limited offensive. The Communist Chinese, as we found out from the China News Service May 1989, at the time had 320,000 troops in North Vietnam.[25] An American invasion would have encountered Red Chinese troops with unknown consequences.

Who could argue with Westmoreland's assertion that public opinion needed to be led by the president, and LBJ should have made the effort to convince the American people and Congress of what needed to be done?[26] Westmoreland admits that limiting American officers to a one-year tour of duty was probably a mistake.[27]

Hackworth points out that "the policy only prevented a man from becoming a good commander" because he was not given enough time in the field.[28]

Summers refers to Vietnam as a "tactical victory" but a "strategic defeat."[29] Summers said to a North Vietnamese colonel after the war: "You know, you never defeated us on the battlefield."

The communist responded, "That may be so, but it is also irrelevant."[30]

Hackworth disagrees with Summers. The Americans, he writes, used tactically "unimaginative hammer-and-anvil operations."[31]

The casualties we inflicted on the NVA did not, he believed, compensate for the losses we took.[32] Hackworth developed his own approach in the field, and it worked. First, he would locate an enemy force and then he would place troops on likely enemy escape routes. Only then would he attack. Air and artillery would smash the enemy's positions and when they tried to escape, they would run right into American ambushes. Typically, this would result in high enemy and low friendly losses. One of Hackworth's operations netted 113 NVA soldiers killed to four Americans slightly wounded.[33] Despite his success, Hackworth could not get the American military to adopt his tactics, even though the Rand Corporation's analysis agreed with him.[34]

Krulak's pacification plan couldn't and didn't work because you just can't ignore the enemy, and U.S. airpower was unable to stop communist infiltration from the North.

Outside of America physically conquering North Vietnam, did the Reds have a breaking point? If a million dead, and millions of wounded soldiers and untold civilian casualties didn't convince them to quit, what would?[35] Krulak calculated that the enemy had at any one time, a pool of about 2.5 million men in Vietnam.[36] The North Vietnamese and Viet Cong were willing "to accept unlimited losses to achieve" reunification of Vietnam.[37] Consequently, the United States would have had to concentrate enough power to destroy this reserve of troops. This would have necessitated a tremendous mobilization of U.S. assets. While not impossible politically, this would have been difficult to achieve militarily, and what would the Red Chinese and Soviets have done in response?

What if the United States had prepared the American people, committed everything we could, bombed North Vietnam to smithereens, used Hackworth's tactics and Krulak's pacification plan?

We come back to Fall's analysis. To win the war we had to deny the communists their sanctuary and win over the Vietnamese peasants. And if we did win, would our victory have been worth the amount of American resources it would have taken, given, as Eisenhower pointed out, that our real enemy in the area was Marxist China?

While the fighting was going on in Vietnam, a thaw was developing in the Cold War. Johnson's foreign policy was tangled in the jungles of Vietnam during 1968 and it took a new president, Nixon, with a different approach, to move American interests ahead again. Nixon was able to improve relations with Red China and the Soviet Union. This fundamentally shifted the pattern of the Cold War. Kissinger made a secret trip to Peking in July 1971 to explore the possibility of the United States' recognition of mainland China.[38] This led to Nixon's visit to Communist China seven months later. The United States and Red China agreed to scientific and cultural exchanges, steps toward the resumption of trade and the eventual reunification of the island of Taiwan with mainland China.[39] Nixon's initiative paved the way for the formal recognition of Marxist China on January 1, 1979.[40] The USSR became worried about U.S.-China relations, which was Nixon's intent, and sought closer ties with America.

During May 1972, Nixon announced that he was going to Moscow.[41] What became known as *détente*, was agreed upon during Nixon's visit. The Soviets promised a more orderly and restrained competition between the two superpowers, and Nixon and Soviet Leader Leonid Brezhnev signed the Strategic Arms Limitation Talks agreement. This treaty limited the number of intercontinental ballistic missiles and anti-ballistic missile systems the two sides could possess. There were also trade agreements, which included grain shipments to the USSR.

After Nixon resigned, Ford continued his policies. In 1974, Ford met with Brezhnev in Vladivostok and they accepted the framework that was to be the basis for SALT II.[42]

When Jimmy Carter became president two years later, the Soviets sensing weakness became more aggressive, supporting Marxist operations in Central America and Africa, and expanding their military capability. The Soviet invasion of Afghanistan in December 1979 led to Carter shelving SALT II, suspending grain shipments to the USSR and organizing a boycott of the 1980 Summer Olympic games in Moscow.[43]

Ronald Reagan was elected president in 1980 and began a huge build-up of American forces in response to the Soviet's military expansion. Reagan said that Communism was finished and its "last pages" were being written.[44] Few believed his pronouncement at the time.

It was during George H. W. Bush's administration (1989-1993) that the Soviet Union would finally collapse, ending the Cold War. The USSR had become overextended with its overseas commitments to Cuba, Central America, Africa, Asia and Afghanistan. That regime had also embarked on a gigantic expansion of its military. Meanwhile, the Soviet economy was about to collapse.

The new head of the Soviet Union, Mikhail Gorbachev, tried to stave off disaster by reforming the communist system, cutting back on the Soviet military and reducing his country's foreign commitments. Gorbachev stopped the Soviets' naval building program, reduced aid to other Marxists, and ordered a withdrawal from Afghanistan in 1989. In July 1989, he said that the Soviets would no longer interfere "in the internal affairs of other states."

Red rule ended peacefully, first in Poland and Hungary, and then in Czechoslovakia and Bulgaria. The people of Romania, however, overthrew their government in a bloodbath. The Berlin Wall fell November 9, 1989[45] and communist East Germany collapsed. This led to the reunification of Germany the next year.[46] A group of political and military leaders on August 18, 1991 tried to seize power from Gorbachev. Boris Yeltsin and Gorbachev defied the coup leaders and the plot failed.[47] The defeat of this attempted takeover resulted in an acceleration of change. Most of the fifteen Soviet Republics declared their independence. On December 8, 1991, Russia, Belarus, and Ukraine announced that the Soviet Union no longer existed. Gorbachev resigned Christmas Day and the Soviets' blood-red Hammer and Sickle flag was lowered for the last time over the Kremlin.[48]

Containment was successful. The Cold War was over. The tale is told.

February 21, 2002.
Mark A. Cauble

Endnotes

Overture: Part I
The Slippery Slope

[1] Robert C. Tucker, ed., *The Marx-Engels Reader* (New York: W.W. Norton & Co., Inc., 1972), 336, 346, 352-353.

[2] Ibid., 537.

[3] David MacKenzie and Michael W. Curran, *A History of the Soviet Union* (Belmont, CA: Wadsworth Publishing Co., 1986), 143-153.

[4] Norman Friedman, *The Fifty Year War: Conflict and Strategy in the Cold War* (Annapolis, MD: Naval Institute Press, 2000), 8.

[5] Winston S. Churchill, *The Second World War: The Gathering Storm* (Boston: Houghton Mifflin Co., 1948), 392.

[6] C.L. Sulzberger, *The American Heritage Picture History of World War II* (American Heritage Publishing Co., Inc. 1966), 61.

[7] Winston S. Churchill, *The Second World War: The Grand Alliance* (Boston: Houghton Mifflin Co., 1950), 377.

[8] Winston S. Churchill, *The Second World War: Triumph and Tragedy* (Boston: Houghton Mifflin Co., 1953), 572-574.

[9] Edward H. Judge and John W. Langdon, *The Cold War: A History Through Documents* (Upper Saddle River, NJ: Prentice Hall, 1999), 33, 35.

[10] Jeremy Isaacs, *Cold War: An Illustrated History, 1945-1991* (Boston: Little, Brown and Co., 1998), 30-34, 38-41, 72-80, 85-87, 86-105, 128, 136-143, 186-187.

[11] Joseph Buttinger, *The Smaller Dragon: A Political History of Vietnam* (New Yorker: Frederick A. Praeger, 1958), 208.

[12] Ibid., 380.

[13] Ibid., 439.

[14] Stanley Karnow, *Vietnam: A History* (New York: Penguin Books, 1997), 146.

[15] Id. *The Smaller Dragon: A Political History of Vietnam,* 446-453.

[16] Bernard B. Fall, *Hell in a Very Small Place: The Siege of Dien Bien Phu* (New York: Da Capo Press, 1966), 133, 410.

[17] Ibid., 312.

[18] Ibid., 455, 459.

[19] Bernard B. Fall, *Street without Joy* (Mechanicsburg, PA: Stackpole Books, 1994), 385.

[20] Id., *Vietnam*, 221.

[21] Id., *Vietnam*, 197-198.

[22] Id., *Street without Joy*, 312.

[23] Id., *Vietnam*, 219-221.

[24] Id., *Vietnam*, 239.

[25] Id., *Vietnam*, 245.

[26] Id., *Vietnam*, 265.

[27] Id., *Vietnam*, 270.

[28] Id., *Vietnam*, 320.

[29] Id., *Vietnam*, 324.

[30] Id., *Vietnam*, 346-347.

[31] Id., *Street without Joy*, 375-382.

[32] Id., *Vietnam*, 195.

[33] Id., *Vietnam*, 494.

[34] David H. Hackworth, *About Face* (New York: Simon & Schuster, 1989), 488, 560, 610.

[35] Id., *Vietnam*, 494-495, 646.

[36] Id., *Vietnam*, 496.

[37] Id., *Vietnam*, 494.

[38] Neil Sheehan, *A Bright Shining Lie: John Paul Vann and America in Vietnam* (New York: Vintage Books, 1988), 629.

[39] Ibid., 630.

[40] Ibid., 631.

[41] Ibid., 632.

[42] Ibid., 636.

[43] Ibid., 638.

[44] Ibid., 651.

[45] Ibid., 640-641.

[46] Ibid., 642.

[47] Ibid., 643.

[48] Ibid., 643-649.

[49] Ibid., 649.

Into the DMZ: Part II
Chapter 1: "We Might See Some Action"

[1] Cauble memoirs

[2] Gary L. Telfer, Lane Rogers and V. Keith Fleming, *U.S. Marines in Vietnam: Fighting the North Vietnamese 1967* (Washington, D.C.: Superintendent of Documents, U.S. Government Printing Office, 1984), 20.

[3] Ibid., 21.

[4] Ibid., 22.

[5] Ibid., 23.

[6] Ibid., 20.

[7] Captain Frank D. Fulford interview by Staff Sergeant James B. Snider at Phu Bai on June 25, 1967

[8] Cauble memoirs

[9] Billy Mitchell memoir May 14, 1967

[10] Jerry Dallape memoirs Nov. 27, 2000, *The Battle of An Hoa* [on-line]; available at http://docrainman.tripod.com/battle.html.

[11] Cauble, letter May 15, 1967.

[12] Charles D. Melson, *U.S. Marine Rifleman in Vietnam 1965-1973* (London: Reed Consumer Books Ltd., 1998), 16-17; Cauble memoirs.

[13] 2/26 "After Action Report," May 1967, Organizational Data 4, Average Monthly Strength

[14] Mitchell memoirs introduction

[15] *Guidebook for Marines* (Washington, DC: Leatherneck Association, Inc., 1962), 4; Id., *U.S. Marine Rifleman in Vietnam, 1965-1973*, 3.

[16] Id., *U.S. Marine Rifleman in Vietnam, 1965-1973*, 7, 11.

[17] Id., *U.S. Marine Rifleman in Vietnam, 1965-1973*, 12.

[18] Oots interview

[19] Command Chronology 2/26, part I g

[20] Command Chronology 2/26, p. 6

[21] Id., *U.S. Marine Rifleman in Vietnam, 1965-1973*, 59.

[22] Captain Oots Interview

[23] Mitchell, May 14, 2000; Mitchell memoirs.

[24] Id., *The Battle of An Hoa.*

[25] Mitchell, May 15

[26] Interview with Major James H. Landers by Staff Sergeant James B. Snider, June 24, 1967, Phu Pai ; Id., *U.S.Marines in Vietnam*, 277.

[27] Command Chronology 2/26 Part II, May 1967

[28] Fulford interview

[29] Id., *The Battle of An Hoa.*

[30] Hancock E-mail, December 2, 2000

[31] Fulford interview

[32] Fulford interview; Id., *U.S. Marine Rifleman in Vietnam, 1965-1973*, 291.

[33] Id., *U.S. Marine Rifleman in Vietnam, 1965-1973*, 291.

[34] Id., *U.S. Marine Rifleman in Vietnam, 1965-1973*, 290.

[35] Command Chronology 2/26, 1. Operations, May 1967

[36] Fulford Interview

[37] Joe Francis e-mail, Oct. 15, 2000

Chapter 2: "Fix Bayonets and Stand By for Action"

[1] Command Chronology 2/9 Operation Hickory, Intelligence 7E

[2] Cauble memoirs

[3] Command Chronology 2/9, May 1967

[4] Cauble memoir

[5] Id., *U.S. Marine Rifleman in Vietnam, 1965-1973*, 24.

[6] Cauble memoirs

[7] Landers interview

[8] Fulford interview

[9] Id., *The Battle of An Hoa*.

[10] Fulford interview, Cauble memoirs

[11] Mitchell memoirs, May 16, 2000.

[12] Cauble memoirs, May 16, 2000; Sheehan, p. 642

[13] Fulford interview

[14] Mitchell memoirs, May 16, 2000.

[15] Fulford interview

[16] Ibid.

[17] Landers interview, taped historical interview documentation sheet 9. Glossary 1m.

[18] Command Chronology 2/26, May 1967

[19] Fulford interview

[20] Platoon diary, May 16, 1967; John D. Giordano Echo 2/26; *The Church at An Hoa* (1998) [database on-line]; available at WashingtonPost.com.

[21] Command Chronology 2/26, May 1967, Combat Air Support 1.C.

[22] Id., *U.S. Marines in Vietnam*, 26.

[23] Fulford interview

[24] Ibid.

[25] Joe Francis e-mail, Oct. 15, 2000

[26] Brown e-mail, Jan. 27, 2000

[27] Fosmo e-mail, Jan. 9, 2000

[28] Ibid., Oct. 19, 2000

[29] Michael Lee Lanning and Dan Cragg, *Inside the VC and the NVA: the Real Story of North Vietnam's Armed Forces* (New York: Fawcett Columbine, 1992), 83.

[30] Command Chronology 2/9, Annex C. 29

[31] Id., *U.S. Marines in Vietnam*, 26; Command Chronology 2/9, 2.a. (2)

[32] First Platoon Diary, Golf Company, May 16

[33] Id., *Inside the VC and the NVA*, 83.

[34] Id., *Inside the VC and the NVA*, 83; William Darryl Henderson, *Why the Viet Cong Fought* (Westport, CT: Greenwood Press, 1979), 34.

[35] Id., *Inside the VC and the NVA*, 101-109.

[36] Oots interview

[37] Command Chronology 3/4, May 1967, Section 3

[38] Command Chronology 3/4, May 1967, Section II 1.b

[39] Fulford interview

[40] Command Chronology 3/4, May 1967, Section III 1.b

[41] Oots interview

[42] Bill Hancock e-mail, Dec. 2, 2000

[43] Douglas Pike, *PAVN: People's Army of Vietnam* (New York: A Da Capo Paperback, 1986), 1.

[44] Id., *Inside the VC and the NVA*, 41.

[45] Id., *Inside the VC and the NVA*, 175; M. Andersen, M. Arnsten and H. Averch, *Insurgent Organization and Operations: a Case Study of the Viet Cong in the Delta, 1964-1966* (Santa Monica, CA: The Rand Corp., 1967), 89-95.

[46] Fulford interview

[47] Id., *The Battle of An Hoa.*

[48] Cauble memoirs

[49] Rainman e-mail, Nov. 16, 2000

[50] Cauble memoirs

[51] Ron Wickersham e-mail, Feb. 20, 2001

[52] Joe Francis letter to Faulkner Family, Dec. 2, 2000

[53] Ibid., Dec. 1, 2000

[54] Id., *The Battle of An Hoa.*

[55] Silver Star citation for Lance Corporal David A. Fisch USMC

[56] Id., *The Battle of An Hoa.*

[57] Navy Cross citation: Corporal Ronald T. Curly

[58] Joe Francis e-mail, Oct. 15, 2000

[59] Id., *The Battle of An Hoa.*

[60] Fulford interview

[61] Ibid.

[62] Captain Oots interview

[63] Fulford interview

[64] Mitchell memoirs, May 16

[65] Command Chronology 2/26, May 1967, Combat Air Support 1.C.

[66] Command Chronology 2/26, May 16

[67] Id., *The Battle of An Hoa.*

[68] Command Chronology 2/26, May 1967, Air Support 1.C., Fire Support and Fire Support Coordination 5.h. Combat Air support. Summary b. After Action Report 2/26, May 1967, 14

[69] Oots interview

[70] Landers, Fulford interview

[71] After Action Report 2/26, May 1967, 14

[72] Ibid., 12

[73] Ibid., 13

[74] Mitchell memoirs May 16

[75] Command Chronology 2/26, May 1967

[76] Captain Oots interview

[77] Richard Ross memoirs, Cauble memoirs

[78] Mitchell memoir, May 16

[79] Cauble memoir

[80] Mitchell memoir, May 16

[81] Cauble memoirs

[82] Mitchell memoirs

[83] Cauble memoirs

[84] Mitchell, May 16

[85] Cauble memoirs

[86] Platoon Diary, May 16

[87] Cauble memoirs

[88] Richard Ross memoirs

[89] Mitchell memoirs, May 16

[90] Cauble memoirs

[91] Mitchell memoirs, May 16

[92] Ross memoirs, Cauble memoirs

93 Mitchell memoirs, May 16
94 Cauble memoirs
95 Platoon Diary, May 16
96 Mitchell memoirs, May 16
97 Citation for Silver Star
98 Cauble memoirs
99 Navy Cross Citation
100 Cauble; Ross; Brown
101 Cauble memoirs; Ross memoirs
102 Mitchell memoirs
103 Id., *The Battle of An Hoa.*
104 Mitchell memoirs
105 Cauble memoirs
106 Mitchell memoirs
107 Bronze Star Citation Brown
108 Brown email, Jan. 27, 2000
109 Bronze Star Citation
110 Bronze Star citation
111 Mitchell memoir, May 16
112 Navy Cross citation
113 Silver Star citation
114 *The Church at An Hoa* (1998) [database on-line]; available at WashingtonPost.com.
115 Cauble memoirs
116 Command Chronology 2/26, part I h.; Cauble memoirs; Id., *The Church at An Hoa*; Brown e-mail, 1/2/2000; Bill Hancock e-mail, 11/30/2000; Wickersham e-mail.
117 Id., *The Church at An Hoa*; Cauble memoirs; UPI, "Yanks Still Hold Besieged Outpost, But Marine Rescuers Pull Back," *Los Angeles Herald Examiner*, 17 May 1967, sec. A, p. 4.
118 Cauble memoirs
119 Oots interview
120 Fulford interview
121 Cauble memoirs
122 Id., *Washington Post*, 2-3.
123 Mitchell memoirs, May 16; Cauble memoirs
124 Landers interview
125 Mitchell memoirs, May 16

[126] Bill Hancock email, Nov. 30, 2000

[127] Fulford interview

[128] Hancock email, Nov. 30, 2000

[129] Mitchell memoir, May 16

[130] Oots interview; Mitchell memoirs; Command Chronology, May 1967

[131] Hancock email, Nov. 30, 2000

[132] Webster e-mail, Jan. 10, 2000

[133] Chicoine letter, 11/1/67

[134] Fulford interview; Oots interview; Ron Wickersham e-mail, Feb. 20, 2001

[135] Id., *U.S. Marines in Vietnam*, 26.

[136] Id., *Los Angeles Herald Examiner*, 4.

[137] Command Chronology 2/26, May 16, 1967

[138] Cauble memoirs; Ross L. Webster email, January 10, 2000; Bill Hancock email, Nov. 30, 2000.

Chapter 3: "Much Bravery Shown Today"

[1] The Associated Press, "Enemy Threatens a Marine Outpost Near Buffer Zone," *New York Times*, 17 May 1967, sec. A, p. 1.

[2] "The War: Demilitarizing the Zone," *Time*, 26 May 1967, 20-21.

[3] Hancock e-mail, Nov. 30, 2000

[4] Platoon Diary; Oots interview

[5] Cauble memoirs

[6] After Action Report 2/26, May 1967, p. 12

[7] Cauble memoirs

[8] Oots interview

[9] FMFM 6-3 1964 figure 40. —Frontal Attack, p. 229

[10] Landers interview; Oots interview; Fulford interview

[11] Oots interview

[12] Fulford interview

[13] Ibid.

[14] Platoon Diary, May 17, 1967

[15] Cauble memoirs

[16] Fulford interview

[17] Oots interview

[18] Cauble memoirs

[19] Oots interview

[20] Ibid.

[21] Cauble memoirs

[22] Oots interview

[23] Ibid.

[24] Fulford interview

[25] Id., *Inside the VC and the NVA*, 175.

[26] David Hackworth, *Military Operations, Vietnam Primer: Lessons Learned* (Washington, DC: Headquarters, Dept. of the Army, 1997), 9-10.

[27] Fulford interview

[28] Cauble memoirs

[29] Oots interview

[30] Fulford interview

[31] Oots interview; Fulford interview

[32] Captain Oots interview

[33] Fulford interview

[34] Mitchell memoirs, May 17; Cauble memoirs

[35] Platoon Diary, May 17

[36] Cauble memoirs

[37] Platoon Diary, May 17

[38] Cauble memoirs

[39] Platoon Diary, May 17

[40] Cauble memoirs

[41] Captain Oots interview

[42] Platoon Diary, May 17

[43] Mitchell's memoirs, May 17

[44] Platoon Diary, May 17

[45] Mitchell memoirs, Navy Cross and Silver Star Citations

[46] Navy Cross Citation

[47] Ibid.

[48] Silver Star citation

[49] Fulford interview

[50] Command Chronology 2/26, May 17, 1967

[51] Ron Wickersham E-mail, Feb. 20, 2001

[52] Fosmo e-mail, Oct. 18, 2000

[53] Ibid., Oct. 19, 2000

[54] Fulford interview

[55] Ibid.

[56] Platoon Diary, May 17

[57] Cauble memoirs

[58] Command Chronology 2/26, May 17, 1967

[59] Cauble memoirs

[60] Silver Star Citation

[61] After Action Report 2/9, 8 Mission, p. 4; Command Chronology 2/9; Operation Hickory 9. Concept of Operation

[62] http://4mermarine.com/USMC/dictionary.html#L

[63] John Murphy's e-mail, June 20, 2003

[64] Id., *U.S. Marines in Vietnam*, 26; Command Chronology 2/9, Operation Hickory 10. Evacuation 9. May 17 to May 18

[65] Id., *U.S. Marines in Vietnam*, 28.

[66] Id., *U.S. Marines in Vietnam*, 26.

[67] Masterpool interview

[68] Fulford interview; Mitchell memoir; Command Chronology 2/26, May 17, 1967

[69] Command Chronology 2/26, May 17, 1967

[70] Cauble memoirs

[71] Platoon Diary, May 17

[72] Command Chronology 2/26, May 17, 1967

[73] Cauble memoirs, Purple Heart Citation

Chapter 4: "Helpless Under the Mortar Fire"

[1] Id., *U.S. Marines in Vietnam*, 26.

[2] Command Chronology 2/26, May 17

[3] Platoon Diary, May 18

[4] Fulford interview; Oots interview

[5] Cauble memoirs

[6] Command Chronology 3/4, May 1-16 Part III 1.g ; Command Chronology 3/4, May 17-31, 10.9, 4

[7] Command Chronology 3/4, May 17-31, 46

[8] Id., *U.S. Marines in Vietnam*, 26.

[9] Mitchell memoirs, May 18

[10] Command Chronology 2/26, May 18, 1967

[11] Command Chronology 2/26, May 18, 1967

[12] Mitchell memoirs, May 18

[13] William L. Myers, *Honor the Warrior: the United States Marine Corps in Vietnam* (Lafayette, LA: Redoubt Press, 2000), 283.

[14] Oots interview

[15] Fulford interview; Command Chronology 2/26, May 18, 1967

[16] Silver Star Citation

[17] Fulford interview

[18] Cauble memoirs

[19] Mitchell, May 18

[20] Cauble memoirs

[21] Mitchell memoirs

[22] Ibid.

[23] Platoon Diary, May 18

[24] Mitchellmemoirs

[25] Mitchell memoirs, May 18

[26] Chicoine letter, 11/1/67

[27] Oots interview

[28] Fulford interview

[29] Id., *U.S. Marines in Vietnam*, 26.

[30] Cauble; Mitchell; Brown memoirs

[31] Fulford interview; Command Chronology 2/9, May 18; FMFM 6-3 1964, 229

[32] Mitchell memoirs, May 18

[33] Cauble memoirs

[34] Ibid.

[35] Mitchell memoirs, May 18

[36] Cauble memoirs

[37] Mitchell memoirs

[38] Cauble memoirs

[39] Mitchell memoirs, May 18; Id., *U.S. Marines in Vietnam*, 26; Although the USMC History confuses what happened on May 18 as having happened on May 19, there was no considerable contact on May 19; Oots interview; Fulford interview; Cauble memoirs; Mitchell memoirs; Command Chronology 2/26, May 18 and 19

[40] Command Chronology 2/9, May 18

[41] Fulford interview

[42] Command Chronology 2/9, May 18

[43] Command Chronology 2/26, May 18

[44] After Action Report 2/9 6.(9)

[45] Cauble memoirs

[46] Cauble; Mitchell memoirs

Chapter 5: "We Were Like Sitting Ducks"

[1] Oots interview; Fulford interview; Id., *U.S. Marines in Vietnam*, 28.

[2] Command Chronology 2/26, May 1967; Intelligence 2.b and Command Chronology 2/9, May 1967 2.b.(1)

[3] Fosmo e-mail, Oct 18, 2000

[4] Cauble memoirs

[5] Fulford interview

[6] 2/26 Command Chronology, May 19

[7] Brown e-mail, Jan. 27, 2000; Susan Freudenheim, "A Window on the War," *Los Angeles Times*, 8 Dec. 2002, sec. E, 50-51.

[8] Cauble memoirs; Brown e-mail, Jan. 27, 2000; Id., "A Window on the War"

[9] Cauble memoirs

[10] Staff Sgt. Russ Havourd, "Lens Girl Faces Peril to 'Make It,'" *Stars and Stripes*, June 1967

[11] Brown e-mail, Jan. 27, 2000; Id., "A Window on the War"

[12] Havourd, "Lens Girl"

[13] Id., "A Window on the War"

[14] Cauble memoirs

[15] Silver Star Citation

[16] Command Chronology 2/26, May 19

[17] Cauble memoirs; Mitchell memoirs, May 19

[18] Fulford interview

[19] Command Chronology 2/26, May 19

[20] Fulford interview

[21] Command Chronology 2/26, May 19

[22] Command Chronology; After Action Report 2/9, May 19

[23] Silver Star Citation

[24] Ibid.

[25] Command Chronology; After Action Report 2/9, May 19

[26] Platoon Diary; Cauble memoirs; Mitchell memoirs

[27] Command Chronology 2/26, May 16-19

[28] Cauble memoirs

Chapter 6:
"Calmly Accepting the Consequences of Their Action"

[1] After Action Report 2/9, May 20; Command Chronology 2/26, May 20

[2] Platoon Diary, May 20 & May 21

[3] Ross L. Webster e-mail, Jan. 10, 2000; Mitchell memoirs, May 20

[4] Id., *U.S. Marines in Vietnam*, 28.

[5] Id., *U.S. Marines in Vietnam*, 28.

[6] Silver Star Citation

[7] Id., *U.S. Marines in Vietnam*, 28.

[8] Navy Cross Citation

[9] Ibid.

[10] Id., *U.S. Marines in Vietnam*, 28.

Chapter 7: "Into the DMZ"

[1] Id., *U.S. Marines in Vietnam, 28.*

[2] Cauble memoirs

[3] Id., *U.S. Marines in Vietnam*, 28.

[4] Oots interview; After Action Report 2/9, May 22

[5] Platoon Diary, May 22

[6] Platoon Diary, May 22; Oots interview

[7] Fulford interview; Cauble memoirs

[8] Fulford interview

[9] Command Chronology 2/26, May 22-24

[10] Mitchell memoirs, May 23

[11] Chicoine letter, Nov. 1, 1967

[12] Cauble memoirs

[13] Command Chronology 2/26, June 20, 1967; Platoon Diary, June 19, 1967

[14] Cauble memoirs

[15] Ibid.

Chapter 8: Hill 117

[1] Tom Lehner's e-mail, Jan. 22, 2001.

[2] Hancock e-mail, Dec. 2, 2000

[3] Chicoine letter, 11/1/67

[4] Id., *U.S. Marines in Vietnam*, 29.

[5] Tom Lehner's e-mail, Jan. 22, 2001

[6] Chicoine letter, 11/1/67

[7] Hancock e-mail, Dec. 2, 2000

[8] Tom Lehner's e-mail, Jan. 22, 2001

[9] Ibid.

[10] Id., *U.S. Marines in Vietnam*, 29.

[11] Id., *U.S. Marines in Vietnam*, 29.

[12] Hancock e-mail, Dec. 2, 2000

[13] Chicoine letter, 11/1/67

[14] Id., *U.S. Marines in Vietnam*, 29.

[15] Masterpool interview

[16] Fulford interview; Masterpool interview

[17] Cauble memoirs

[18] Hancock e-mail, Dec. 2, 2000

[19] Chicoine letter, 11/1/67

[20] Id., *U.S. Marines in Vietnam*, 29; Chicoine letter, 11/1/67

[21] Masterpool interview; Id., *U.S. Marines in Vietnam*, 29.

[22] Masterpool interview

[23] Id., *U.S. Marines in Vietnam*, 29.

[24] Command Chronology 2/26, May 26

[25] Id., *U.S. Marines in Vietnam*, 29.

[26] Fulford interview

[27] Command Chronology 2/26, May 27

[28] Id., *U.S. Marines in Vietnam*, 29.

[29] Cauble memoirs

Chapter 9: "Men Are About Pooped"

[1] Platoon Diary, May 27

[2] Id., *U.S. Marines in Vietnam*, 29; Command Chronology 2/26, May 27

[3] Cauble memoirs

[4] Chaplin e-mail, April 27, 2001

[5] Command Chronology 2/26, May 28

[6] Fulford interview

[7] Id., *U.S. Marines in Vietnam*, 30; Command Chronology 2/26, May 28

[8] Captain Oots interview

[9] Mitchell memoirs; Platoon Diary

[10] Cauble memoirs; Mitchell memoirs; Platoon Diary; Command Chronology 2/26, May 31

[11] Id., *U.S. Marines in Vietnam*, 30.

[12] Id., *U.S. Marines in Vietnam*, 30; Platoon Diary; Mitchell memoirs

[13] Cauble memoirs; Mitchell memoirs; Platoon Diary

[14] Platoon Diary; Oots interview

[15] Fulford interview

[16] Cauble memoirs

[17] Platoon Diary; Fulford interview

[18] Command Chronology 2/26, May 1967
[19] Platoon Diary, July 3, 1967
[20] Cauble memoirs; Chaplin email, April 27, 2001

Chapter 10: "He Was a Good Captain"
[1] Platoon Diary; Oots interview
[2] Cauble memoirs
[3] Platoon Diary, June 5
[4] Ron Wickersham e-mail, Feb. 20, 2001
[5] Platoon Diary June 8; Mitchell memoirs
[6] Platoon Diary, June 9
[7] Chicoine letter, 11/1/67, Presidential Unit Citation
[8] Platoon Diary, June 10
[9] Id., *Vietnam*, 552-555.
[10] Mitchell memoirs
[11] Cauble memoirs; Ross phone conversation

Epilogue: Part III
End Game
[1] Id., *U.S. Marines in Vietnam*, 95-96.
[2] Id., *Vietnam*, 530.
[3] Westmoreland, p. 436
[4] Herbert Y. Schandler, *Lyndon Johnson and Vietnam: The Unmaking of a President* (Princeton, NJ: Princeton Univ. Press, 1977), 198-199.
[5] Id., *Lyndon Johnson and Vietnam*, 197.
[6] Michael Maclear, *The Ten Thousand Day War: Vietnam, 1945-1975* (New York: Avon Books, 1981), 199.
[7] Id., *Lyndon Johnson and Vietnam*, 222.
[8] Id., *Lyndon Johnson and Vietnam*, 219.
[9] Clark Clifford, *Counsel to the President: a Memoir* (New York: Anchor Books, 1991), 502.
[10] Id., *Counsel to the President*, 505.
[11] Id., *Vietnam*, 580-581.
[12] Richard M. Nixon, *RN: the Memoirs of Richard Nixon* (New York: A Touchstone Book, 1990), 351.
[13] Id., *RN*, 298; Id., *Vietnam*, 669.
[14] Id., *RN*, 348.
[15] Id., *Vietnam*, 657.

[16] Id., *Vietnam*, 655.

[17] Henry Kissinger, *White House Years* (Boston: Little, Brown and Co., 1979), 1341-1359.

[18] Id., *Ten Thousand Day War*, 308-309.

[19] Id., *The Ten Thousand Day War*, 310.

[20] Id., *Vietnam*, 23, 59.

[21] Id., *RN*, 889; Id., *White House Years*, 1359; William C. Westmoreland, *A Soldier Reports* (New York: Dell Publishing, 1980), 539.

[22] Id., *A Soldier Reports*, 542.

[23] Harry G. Summers, *On Strategy: The Vietnam War in Context* (Carlisle Barracks, PA: Strategic Studies Institute, U.S. Army War College, 1982), 73-76.

[24] Id., *A Soldier Reports*, 543.

[25] "Chinese Troops Fought U.S. in Vietnam," *The Washington Times*, 17 June 1989, sec. A, p. 10.

[26] Id., *A Soldier Reports*, 545.

[27] Id., *A Soldier Reports*, 551.

[28] Id., *About Face*, 484-485.

[29] Id., *On Strategy*, 1.

[30] Id., *Vietnam*, 19.

[31] Id., *About Face*, 554.

[32] Id., *About Face*, 508-509.

[33] Id., *About Face*, 702-703.

[34] Id., *Insurgent Organization and Operations*, 95.

[35] Id., *Vietnam*, 23.

[36] Id., *A Bright Shining Lie*, 630.

[37] Id., *Vietnam*, 20-21.

[38] Id., *White House Years*, 740-755.

[39] Id., *White House Years*, 1053-1096.

[40] Documents, p. 186

[41] Id., *White House Years*, 1197-1198.

[42] Documents, 170-171

[43] Documents, 198-200

[44] Documents, 206

[45] Documents, 245

[46] Documents, 248

[47] Documents, 256-261

[48] Documents, 261-263

Bibliography

Anderson, M., M. Arnsten, and H. Averch. *Insurgent Organization and Operations: A Case Study of the Viet Cong in the Delta, 1964-1966*. Santa Monica: Rand Corporation, 1967. RM-5239-1-ISA/ARPA.

Buttinger, Joseph. *The Smaller Dragon: A Political History of Vietnam*. New York: Frederick Praeger, 1958.

Churchill, Winston S. *The Second World War: The Gathering Storm*. Boston: Houghton Mifflin Company, 1948.

_____. *The Second World War: The Grand Alliance*. Boston: Houghton Mifflin Company, 1950.

_____. *The Second World War: Triumph and Tragedy*. Boston: Houghton Mifflin Company, 1953.

Clifford, Clark with Richard Holbrooke. *Counsel to the President: A Memoir*. New York: Doubleday, 1991.

Emering, Edward J. *Weapons and Field Gear of the North Vietnamese Army and Viet Cong*. Atglen, PA: Schiffer Publishing Ltd., 1998.

Fall, Bernard B. *Hell in a Very Small Place: The Siege of Dien Bien Phu*. New York: Da Capo, 1966.

_____. *Street Without Joy*. Introduction by George C. Herring. Mechanicsburg, PA: Stackpole Books, 1994.

Friedman, Norman. *The Fifty-Year War: Conflict and Strategy in the Cold War*. Annapolis, MD: Naval Institute Press, 2000.

Gander, Terry. *Anti-Tank Weapons*. Ramsbury, Marlborough: The Crowood Press Ltd., 2000.

Guidebook for Marines. Washington, D.C.: The Leatherneck Association, Inc., 1962.

Hackworth, David H. and Julie Sherman. *About Face*. New York: Simon & Schuster, 1989.

Hackworth, David H. *Military Operations, Lessons Learned: Vietnam Primer*. [Washington, D.C.]: Headquarters, Department of the Army, 1997.

Henderson, William Darryl. *Why the Vietcong Fought: A Study of Motivation and Control in a Modern Army in Combat*. Contributions in Political Science, Number 31. Westport, CT: Greenwood Press, 1979.

Isaacs, Jeremy. *Cold War: an Illustrated History, 1945-1991*. Boston: Little, Brown and Company, 1998.

Judge, Edward H. and John W. Langdon, eds. *The Cold War: A History Through Documents*. Upper Saddle River, NJ: Prentice Hall, 1999.

Karnow, Stanley. *Vietnam: A History*. New York: Penguin Group, 1997.

Kissinger, Henry. *White House Years*. Boston: Little, Brown and Company, 1979.

Lanning, Michael Lee and Dan Cragg. *Inside the VC and the NVA: The Real Story of North Vietnam's Armed Forces*. New York: Fawcett Columbine, 1992.

MacKenzie, David and Michael W. Curran. *A History of the Soviet Union*. Belmont, CA: Wadsworth Publishing Company, 1986.

Maclear, Michael. *The Ten Thousand Day War: Vietnam, 1945-1975*. New York: Avon Books, 1981.

Melson, Charles D. *U.S. Marine Rifleman in Vietnam, 1965-73.* Osprey New Vanguard Series: 23. London: Reed Consumer Books Ltd., 1998.

Myers, William L. *Honor the Warrior: The United States Marine Corps in Vietnam.* Lafayette: Redoubt Press, 2000.

Nixon, Richard M. *RN: The Memoirs of Richard Nixon.* New York: Simon & Schuster, Inc., 1990.

Pike, Douglas. *PAVN: People's Army of Vietnam.* New York: Da Capo Press, Inc., 1986.

Schandler, Herbert Y. *Lyndon Johnson and Vietnam: The Unmaking of a President.* Princeton: Princeton University Press, 1977.

Sheehan, Neil. *A Bright Shining Lie: John Paul Vann and America in Vietnam.* New York: Random House, Inc., 1988.

Sulzberger, C.L. *The American Heritage Picture History of World War II.* [New York]: American Heritage Publishing Co, Inc., 1966.

Summers, Harry G. *On Strategy: The Vietnam War in Context.* Carlisle Barracks, PA: Strategic Studies Institute, U.S. Army War College, 1982.

Telfer, Gary L., Lane Rogers, and V. Keith Fleming. *U.S. Marines in Vietnam: Fighting the North Vietnamese, 1967.* Washington, D.C.: Superintendent of Documents, U.S. Government Printing Office, 1984.

Tucker, Robert C. ed. *The Marx-Engels Reader.* New York: W.W. Norton & Company, Inc., 1972.

Westmoreland, William C. *A Soldier Reports.* New York: Dell Publishing Co., Inc., 1980.

Zaloga, Steven J. *The M47 and M48 Patton Tanks*. Osprey New
    Vanguard Series: 31. United Kingdom: Osprey Publishing Ltd.,
    1999.

E-Mails
Robert Brown to author, Jan. 27, 2000
Duncan D. Chaplin III to author, April 27, 2001
Harold Fosmo, Jr. to author, Oct. 18, 2000, Oct. 19, 2000, Jan. 9,
    2000
Joe Francis to author, Oct. 15, 2000, Dec. 1, 2000
Bill Hancock to author, Nov. 30, 2000, Dec. 2, 2000
John Murphy to author, June 20, 2003
Doc Rainman to author, Nov. 16, 2000
Ross L. Webster to author, Jan. 10, 2000
Ron Wickersham to author, Feb. 20, 2001

Letters
Roger Chicoine to parents, Nov. 1, 1967

Magazine articles
"The War: Demilitarizing the Zone," *Time*, 26 May 1967, 20-21.

Memoirs
Mark Cauble, Memoirs and letters
Jerry Dallape, "The Battle of An Hoa"
Tom Lehner
Billy Mitchell
Richard Ross, Telephone interview with author

Newspaper Articles
AP, "Enemy Threatens a Marine Outpost Near Buffer Zone," *New
    York Times*, 17 May 1967, Sec. A, p. 1.
Stars and Stripes, "Lens Girl Faces Peril to 'Make It,'" June 1967
UPI, "Yanks Still Hold Besieged Outpost, But Marine Rescuers
    Pull Back," *Los Angeles Herald Examiner,* 17 May 1967, Sec.
    A, p. 4.
Washington Post, "The Church at An Hoa" (1998) [Database On-
    line]: Available at Washingtonpost.com

Government Documents

After Action Reports
2/9 After Action Report, Operation Hickory, May 1967. Marine
    Corps Historical Center, Washington, D.C.
2/26 After Action Report, Operation Hickory, May 1967. Marine
    Corps Historical Center, Washington, D.C.

Command Chronologies:
2/9 Command Chronology, May 1967. Marine Corps Historical
    Center, Washington, D.C.
2/26 Command Chronology, May 1967, June 1967. Marine Corps
    Historical Center, Washington, D.C.
3/4 Command Chronology, May 1967. Marine Corps Historical
    Center, Washington, D.C.

First Platoon Diary, Golf Company, 2/26 1967

FMFM 6-3 1964 Manual

Citations
Navy Cross
    Lance Corporal David G. Bendorf
    Corporal Ronald T. Curly
    PFC David E. Hartsoe
    Corporal Richard E. Moffit
Silver Star
    Corporal John C. Chambers
    Lance Corporal David. A. Fisch
    Sergeant William Baxter Gilley
    Corporal Richard K. Gillingham
    Corporal James W. Hart, Jr.
    Gunnery Sergeant Donalano Francisco Martinez
    Second Lieutenant Daniel R. Phipps
    Corporal Walter J. Washut
Bronze Star
    2nd Lieutenant Robert Brown
Presidential Unit Citation Nov. 1, 1967

Taped Interviews

Captain Frank D. Fulford interviewed by Staff Sergeant James B. Snider at Phu Bai, South Vietnam on June 25, 1967. Marine Corps Historical Center, Washington, D.C.

Major James H. Landers interviewed by Staff Sergeant James B. Snider at Phu Bai, South Vietnam on June 24, 1967 with documentation sheet. Marine Corps Historical Center, Washington, D.C.

Lt. Col. William J. Masterpool interviewed by Staff Sergeant James B. Snider June 24, 1967. Marine Corps Historical Center, Washington, D.C.

Captain Samuel Otts interviewed by Staff Sergeant James B. Snider at Phu Bai, South Vietnam on June 25, 1967. Marine Corps Historical Center, Washington, D.C.

Index

Mark and Sue Ann Cauble *(Photo courtesy of Dennis Butcher)*

ABOUT THE AUTHOR

Mark A. Cauble was wounded twice in Vietnam while serving with the 2nd Battalion, 26th Marines. After returning from Vietnam, he went to college and became a history professor. He lives in Southern California with his wife, Sue Ann.